She Won't Be Silenced

by Lisa Freeman

especially for Bill
lizm xx

1

"Our True Crime Books are works of nonfiction. No names have been changed, no characters invented, no events fabricated."

~ RJ Parker Publishing

2

She Won't Be Silenced

by Lisa Freeman

ISBN-13: 978-1987902112
ISBN-10: 1987902114

Copyright and Published
(09.2016)

by

RJ Parker Publishing

http://RJParkerPublishing.com

Published in Canada

10 9 8 7 6 5 4 3 2 1

Copyrights

Table of Contents

I must go down to the seas again, to the lonely sea
and the sky,
And all I ask is a tall ship and a star to steer her by,
And the wheel's kick and the wind's song and the
white sail's shaking,
And a grey mist on the sea's face, and a grey dawn
breaking.
I must go down to the seas again, for the call of the
running tide
Is a wild call and a clear call that may not be
denied;
And all I ask is a windy day with the white clouds
flying,
And the flung spray and the blown spume, and the
sea-gulls crying.
I must go down to the seas again, to the vagrant
gypsy life,
To the gull's way and the whale's way, where the
wind's like a whetted knife;
And all I ask is a merry yarn from a laughing
fellow-rover,
And quiet sleep and a sweet dream when the long
trick's over.

Sea Fever
John Masefield
English Poet

In Memory of Deb and Dad
This is their story too.

And for Mum, CJ & Mad

This is so wrong, so wrong, and I don't want to do it. That I am even at the hospital is a mistake, a fluke, as I had no intention of going there. There was no need -- they have told us Dad is dead. The hospital is somewhere I wish I had to go -- that he was injured somehow, alive still, not gone forever. But Deb and I went to the house on Brock Street to get Caroline. She was hysterical, crying, in denial and shock. She must get into the house, she was demanding; she wanted to see her father.

When Deb and I pulled up, she was screaming at a police officer and he was trying his best to calm her down, which was next to impossible. She was threatening to cross the police barrier to get inside the house, and they told her that she would be arrested if she did. I remember a Supervisor trying to reason with her, her father wasn't there, he told her, his body had already been removed. Well, if she wasn't getting into the house to see Dad, she was going to see him at the hospital. Deb and I tried to make her see sense, but she was determined. Fine, fine, go up to the hospital, just leave the crime scene so you don't get yourself arrested. Little did I know that what would happen at the hospital that night would paint my nightmares red for years to come.

Chapter 1 ~ Traces

The streets of my childhood are still there and I walk down them every day. I don't go by house numbers on these streets; it's the Benson's place, Jack and June's, and other houses with names of families long departed. Same houses, different people. The same buildings and shops are still part of the neighbourhood too, but now with different storefronts and names. The fish store at the end of the road that my father used to help out at sells seafood no more – it's current incarnation is a used car dealership, but it'll always be the Fish Store to me. Generations of this area and the changes they bring with them come and go, but I remain the same.

I liken myself to the different configurations of houses and buildings that are in the area where I grew up and in which I still live – sound and familiar. There have been changes though, and I too have changed. Life has changed me in outward appearance over time, and through marriages I too have had different names. Life experiences have taught me and shaped me, but inside, though, I will always be Lisie, the long ago girl of my childhood.

I walk a couple of streets over from where I now live to have a look at the house I grew up in. It looks tired. Tired, but still standing, and these words, at times, are how I describe myself. The huge defining maple tree that sheltered us from the hot summer sun and the worst of the winter winds has been cut down to a humiliating stump. The front porch steps have been altered, and the beige stucco, without my mother's constant care, is chipped and flaking. The garage still stands, and it at least looks to have had an update through the years. The red roses my Mum had trailed along the back part of the house have long since died away, and the grapevines in the backyard that my father brought with him from his native Niagara are long gone too. After all, it is someone else's house and property now and has been for a long time: it's been almost 20 years since anyone from our family has called the little house on Gladstone home.

I walk along my old street kicking up dry leaves on this crisp fall day and, as I do, my mind wanders. Does a smaller shoe size of my younger self still exist, imprinted somewhere on these pavements of my youth? After all, I've spent half my life running, skipping, and jumping on these sidewalks. Why am I so eager to connect again with that young freckled blonde girl, the one with the ready smile, that happy girl? Do I want to grab her and tell her what is coming? Ready or not, Lisie, life is coming. I would like to warn her, yes, but there is something else. So many things I'd like to tell that girl as she grows up, but most important of them all is that she has to hang on to the part of herself that knows happiness. There will be times when it will be hard to find, and even harder to feel,

10

but it's still there. The wind blows up, whipping the remaining leaves into a little whirlwind on the sidewalk ahead of me. The day has gotten colder, time to shake off my visit to the past and head back home, which is just a few blocks over. I'll come back again soon, though, where I can easily make a connection back to a simpler time in my life when everyone who mattered to me was still in their rightly places in this world.

My world.

Chapter 2 ~ Striking Sixteen Bells

I was weary of winter and it was only the beginning of February. The harshness of the season has set in now that the warmth of Christmas and the revelry of New Year's have since faded. What is left in their wake is stark frozen ground, bare trees, and a slick veneer called ice which coats every surface that I need to tread upon. Winter is a season that seems to last ten times its actual length, but it needn't to if only spring were to start when it was supposed to as noted on the calendar. Here it doesn't, though; it comes at its own choosing, April or sometimes well into May. And here in Southern Ontario, where we are more densely populated than the rest, it is as if we collectively huddle around the Great Lakes for warmth and bide our time.

At least I do anyway.

In the early days of the New Year of 1991, the usual January thaw didn't happen, and the longest cold spell was the week of January 21-28th, with seven consecutive days below freezing. Southern Ontario in the winter can be a nasty place, and it's not unusual for the temperatures to plummet just past Halloween and stay cold for months on end. The cold and freezing days can seem endless: icy and raw and often with wind-chill temperatures that can cut through even the most layered and bundled-up of people. There is a certain coldness to a Canadian winter: a cold that can seep into your bones and make you forget that you ever felt any warmth there. But, I concede, wintertime can be beautiful too. And there is something almost magical when out walking amongst the freshly fallen snow, and the sun striking at the right angle can make it look as if diamond glints have been seemingly dusted on top. To turn and glance behind at the carpet of white, your lone footprints in the snow can make it seem as if you are the only person walking on Earth. And even the starved and barren trees in the winter can be exquisitely beautiful: their branches become full again after a heavy snowfall, laden with weighty loads of snow and ice, bending and twisting and threatening to break with every new gust of wind. Theirs is a delicate balance in which their strength outweighs their fragility; and unbeknownst to me at the time, this would be a future life balance that I would struggle to attain.

What did you do to me, Winter, to make me grieve you so?

The previous summer I had gone off to England by myself, much to the consternation of my mother. I had never flown before, had never even been to the airport, and she was naturally worried that I was doing this all on my own. She thought that perhaps I should take a short flight somewhere first, to see if I would even like flying. No, I said, might as well just set my path for England, and if I didn't like the flight, well, not much I could do about it when I was up there. She

13

need not have worried, not only did I like flying, I discovered a joy of traveling on my own, and my solo adventure to England in May 1990 brought me back to Canada brimming with excitement and plans to return there the following summer. I knew I had found a gem in England's South Downs, and I was barely back on Canadian soil for five minutes when I was already plotting and planning my return visit. The seed had been planted; I was young, unattached, and very much looking forward to the future. So as the summer of 1990 faded into fall and with winter settling upon us, my future plans were clear in my mind: back to England I would go -- all I had to do was to get through the winter.

And my life at that time was just like anyone else's that I hung around with in Oshawa, Ontario, a fair-sized city situated on the Lake Ontario shoreline about 60 kilometres (35 miles) east of Toronto. I was part of a close circle of friends who met up every weekend at the local hockey rink to watch our home team play, then we'd head out for pizza afterwards. We'd think nothing of going all over Ontario to follow the team's road games, or hopping on the GO train into Toronto to watch a NHL game. And if it wasn't my friends I was spending time with, it would be my older sister Deb. Even though she was my elder by seven years, we were very close. There were two younger sisters as well in our family, so there were always lots of places to go and things to do or talk about. And with a house full of girls, there was never any shortage of

14

squabbling and drama, but for the most part we all got along well. But no matter who had a falling-out with whom, if someone from outside the family had something unkind to say about one of us, we would defend our sister no matter what. I've always found this to be our best sisterly trait; no matter what problems we had amongst ourselves, woe to anyone outside the family who would dare badmouth one of us.

A few weeks before that Christmas, our older sister had emergency surgery, and the follow-up tests showed that she had uterine cancer. We were distraught; however, because of how soon they caught it, her doctors were optimistic for the outcome. She was a happy-go-lucky person and very much the glue that held us all together. Not only was she our big sister, but to each of us she would come to mean many things. She never fell out with any of her younger sisters, and it was she who would usually be the voice of reason between the rest of us when we did. And, for whatever reason, we weren't the kind of family who sat down and talked about things, but we knew, and more importantly Deb knew, that we would support her in whatever way we could.

So as the old year ended we looked toward the New Year with some measure of trepidation. All her appointments were slated for early in the year for radiation treatments at one of the best hospitals in the area, Toronto's Sunnybrook Hospital. We were worried, but she had a lot of things going for

15

her in regards to a full recovery. She was young, still in her late twenties at the time, and otherwise a strong and healthy person. Looking back, even with our sister's health issues on the horizon, it is hard to believe there was ever a time when everything was so calm in our lives, so normal, and so very ordinary.

On Tuesday, the 5th of February, I was working at my second job, helping clean the offices of a municipal building in Whitby, which was just the next town over. It was something I did a couple of nights a week, and it was easy work and good money, and any extra money that I could earn would make the proposed trip back to England seem more real. And besides, I had a student loan to pay off -- I had taken a course at Durham College the year before and I had monthly payments of $34.10 to make. The full amount of the loan amount has long since been forgotten, but that meager monthly sum has always stayed in my mind.

Locked away in that building that evening, as the temperature dropped and the night closed in around me, I was unaware that there was a family drama unfolding. So I was more than a bit startled when someone was pounding at the door and calling my name. It was my older sister and she was there a half-hour before our scheduled pick-up time of 10 p.m. As she helped me gather my things, she explained that our Aunt had called both her and our mother explaining that on her way home from an evening out, she had seen something that had her worried. There was yellow crime scene tape cordoning off a house on Brock Street East, near to her own house and a property that she knew my Dad was an on-site caretaker. There was a lot of police presence in the area and she had asked one of the officers posted outside if he could tell her what happened, but he was tight lipped. She didn't know what was going on, but she was troubled. From what I could gather, while I was at the office building in Whitby, my Mum, Aunt and my sister were trying to piece out what bits of information they could get and they were calling around trying to see where Dad was or who had seen him last. So one moment I am emptying wastepaper baskets and the next moment I am in my older sister's car and heading to the police station to see what we could find out.

One very mundane task to an extraordinarily life-changing one.

We made our way to the front lobby of the police station and told an officer at the desk who we were and what little we knew. He interrupted us for a moment and got on the radio to cancel the patrol car that was en route to our family home, explaining to the other officers that we were at the station now. Already I was surprised that this conversation had gone as far as it had: I thought by now we would have been dismissed and sent home and told that our concerns were unfounded. Instead, I could feel a sense of uneasiness start to set in and a subtle shift of displacement.

Certain details are etched in my mind and will always be there while other things have just slipped away. The room Deb and I were taken to was small. Small and sparse, just a desk and a few chairs, a basic police interview room. Maybe they kept things simple in rooms like these so there aren't many distractions and people are able to focus on what is being asked of them or told to them. A man came in and introduced himself as Detective Rod MacDonald. He asked who we were; sisters, we told him, and that we were looking for information. We repeated the story we told at the front desk and what our Aunt had seen at the rental house on Brock Street, which was incidentally just a few blocks away from where we now sat. He probably knew all this anyway and just wanted to hear our account of what we knew. The detective began talking about the property on Brock Street, and he confirmed that it was cordoned off because there had been an incident there, an altercation, and he paused to let his words sink in. I thought at first that my Dad was hurt, hurt badly enough that he would be at the hospital receiving treatment. Then Detective MacDonald said he was sorry to have to tell us this, but there was a fatality at the house and that it was our father.

I sat there not moving, and even though I could hear what he was saying, I could not comprehend it. My father what? He was injured, is that what he meant? Or maybe, as impossible as it may seem, had my Dad injured or killed someone in this altercation? While all these questions are going through my mind, to the right of me I can hear my sister crying, softly sobbing. She was able to absorb what was being told to us right away, while I just couldn't seem to take anything in. When you hear bad news, your mind tries to protect you, numb you, and this is what happened to me. I could hear what was being said to me, but could not absorb it. It was as if everything that was being said was in bubbles floating around my head, not settling anywhere, just drifting past. And when it finally did sink in that the man who was the fatality in the altercation on Brock Street was Dad, our Dad, then my questions did not stop. I couldn't stop asking them because my mind needed answers to cushion the shock of information that it had just received. Who? What? How? Why? I needed details to make it real, so my mind could try to make some sense of it. There was no crying from me, not there, not then, but I had questions and I needed answers. What happened?

Your father was a victim of a brutal assault, we were told, and he died of his injuries. Everything was in its preliminary stages, and the police had more questions than answers themselves at this point. It was very early going, the Detective said, but they had someone in custody, in a holding cell. And his name? I asked. John Terrance Porter. Did the name mean anything to either one of us? No, nothing, we told him, we had never even heard of him. But in the days, weeks, months and years to come, that name would become a monumental one throughout our lives.

Detective MacDonald gave us what few details he had, and looking back, he did his best to shield us from the horror of what happened to our Dad that night as best as he could. I remember him asking us if we needed a ride home or if we were okay to drive. We made it to the car and just sat there, stunned and shocked. There was just such a feeling of unreality to the whole situation and at the same time the sensation that something was slipping away from me, from us. Life as we knew it was over, irreversibly changed, and what we knew weighed heavy between us and the knowledge that in five short minutes and just down the road, we were going to drop a bombshell on our family that would change everything and everyone. A Tuesday that started like every other one before it was ending like no other. We were regular everyday people arriving at the police station that night, but utterly devastated and destroyed people leaving.

Chapter 3 ~ Silent Hours

The unbelievable news from the police station was still to be broken to our mother, our younger sister and the rest of the family, including another sister from our mother's second marriage who had just turned 17 the day before. And who was going to tell Grandma? Our Dad's mother was 92 and living in a nursing home in Niagara-on-the-Lake, and someone had to tell her what happened. Deb was a wreck and I was still trying to take it all in, but at some point our Aunt was back at our house helping out the best she could. Between my Mum and her sister, they seemed to call relatives all over the country with the horrific news and share what few details could be passed along. It didn't matter who was told about what happened, the result was the same: shock and disbelief. It was imperative that family and friends heard it from us before it was in the papers and on the news. Someone called my Dad's sister Violet in Niagara and broke the news to her, and she had the heartbreaking job of telling Grandma. Too late, as we found out later; our Grandmother heard that her son had been murdered when she was listening to the news on her radio in her room at the nursing home.

By far, the very worst person who had to be told about what happened to Dad was our younger sister, Caroline. Where Deb and I were separated by seven years, Caroline is 13 months younger than I am. The task to tell her fell to my mother and my Aunt. I wasn't in the room when they told her, but I could hear her screams of disbelief, and almost from that day forward, we lost a huge part of her. Her pain was not just emotional, it was physical, and she literally was incapacitated for the days, weeks and months that followed. The murder of our father changed all of us, forever changed us in ways that could be immediately seen and in ways that would take years to manifest. But no one took it harder, no one came out of it worse off than Caroline did. She changed completely from that time onward, and throughout the years, she was unable to fully shake off the dark veil of depression that consumed her.

Damn you, John Terrance Porter, whoever you are, for breaking my sister.

*****

God knows, the ambulance crew called out that cold February evening to the house on Brock Street tried their very best to save our Dad. Our family never had the opportunity to thank them, and I wondered if they ever forgot the horrors that they saw on that call-out that long ago winter night. They were there quickly; the call came in from dispatch at 18:32 and they arrived at the house four minutes later and were attending to my father one minute after that. There they found a male, aged 58, lying face down in the snow on the back patio that led to the backyard. His head and neck had acute facial lacerations, his face was flattened, with the left eye swollen shut. They noted wounds to his forehead and that his lower jaw appeared to be broken, as well as a break to the right forearm with bleeding. The paramedics meticulously wrote down their every action that evening in their efforts to resuscitate my Dad.

1837 hrs. - Pt. Rolled onto his back
1838 hrs. - CPR initiated
1840 hrs. - Cardiac monitor in place
1841 hrs. - Defib x2 –200J + 300J CPR continued
1842 hrs. - Second vehicle arrived
1843 hrs.- C. Collon in place Pt. On spine board, moved to vehicle
1846 hrs. - Pt. Suctioned
1847 hrs. - IV attempt left elbow
1847 hrs. - Call to OGH

With lights flashing and sirens cutting through the night, the ambulance arrived at 1850 to the Oshawa General Hospital, with the patient on board showing no vital signs. He was hooked up to a monitor, but no blood pressure, no pulse. His right pupil was fixed and dilated and the left eye closed. The attending physician pronounced death at 1850.

Damn you, John Terrance Porter, whoever

you are, for taking Dad from us.

In the blink of an eye I am eight years old, going into the fish store with my Dad for a treat. Oddly enough, the treat is that wavy ribbon candy that you can only seem to buy at Christmastime. As my adult self looking back, I wonder why it was the only candy the fish store sold? How does wavy multi-coloured ribbon candy tie in with trout, salmon, and lobsters? Do the waves of the candy remind them of the seas and oceans they were plucked from? I don't know, and there's no one left to ask, and I probably wouldn't ask anyway. I don't think other people think the way I do.

Next, I am my teenage self headed down Bond Street past the fish store. I don't see my Dad, but he's trying to get my attention from the other side of the street shouting over the noise of the traffic. He's calling me from the shop's front door: Lisie! Lucy! But I can't hear him over the din. And then I hear LUCINDIA! he's shouting and is waving his arms. I slink across the street, least of all to get him to stop calling out these crazy nicknames of my childhood. I would never be plain old Lisa to him and cannot recall a time actually hearing him call me that. The pet names my father gave to me and my sisters were just as good as our given names and used almost exclusively. We were Deborah, Lisa and Caroline to the world, but Dad referred to us by the special names he gave us, or, to keep it simple, he would collectively refer to us as 'his sons.'

Whenever I go past the old fish store, my mind easily puts him in that doorway again, waving, calling.

The din of the traffic dies down and I pause, hopeful.

Nothing.

I'm at the hospital later that evening to identify my father's body. Or maybe it was past midnight and into the early hours of the morning. I don't know, nor do I need to remember; time meant nothing anymore; there was no beginning or end to things, no chronological order. It was as if I was drifting and I couldn't find a place where I could get my footing again, couldn't find anywhere I felt grounded.

This is so wrong, so wrong, and I don't want to do it. That I am even at the hospital is a mistake, a fluke, as I had no intention of going there. There was no need -- they have told us Dad is dead. The hospital is somewhere I wish I had to go -- that he was injured somehow, alive still, not dead. But Deb and I had to go to the house on Brock Street to get Caroline. She was hysterical, screaming, crying, in denial and shock. She must get into the house, she was demanding; she wanted to see her father. When Deb and I pulled up, she was screaming at a police officer and he was trying his best to calm her down, which, of course, was next to impossible. She was threatening to cross the police barrier to get inside the house, and they told her that she would be arrested if she did. I remember a supervisor trying to reason with her, her father wasn't there, the body had already been removed. Well, if she wasn't getting into the house to see Dad, she was going to see him at the hospital. Deb and I tried to make her see sense, but she was determined. Fine, fine, go up to the hospital, just leave the crime scene so you don't get arrested.

Not that we thought that her being at the hospital was going to be any better, but we were hoping against hope that by the time we got there, maybe she would've calmed down and that we would've been able to talk her round. It didn't happen that way, things escalated instead. Her hysterics at the house on Brock Street just moved a few blocks up the road to the hospital. Not that anyone could blame her, not really. She had just received traumatic news and this was her reaction, her way of coping. She was shouting and screaming at anyone who wouldn't give her what, to her mind, were reasonable answers. She was on the cusp of a complete breakdown, we could see that. Someone called my Aunt, and thank God she came up to the hospital to try to help us out. I think it was a security guard at the hospital who said that if Caroline wanted to see her Dad, let her, then it's done. Someone needed to officially identify the body anyway, he tells us.

But it wouldn't be done and it wouldn't be the end of it, we knew that. Instead it would be the beginning of it and it would destroy her. Out of the four of us girls, she was always the least able to cope with things; she had apprehensiveness in her that didn't seem to be in the rest of us. But short of physically restraining her, she was determined to see him. And as for identifying the body, I was under the impression that someone already did -- a friend of our Dad's. I'm sure somewhere through the course of this never-ending nightmare, someone had told me that. Yes, true, they did, but they still needed someone from the family to do it.

A security guard and a police officer took us to the elevator that would take us down to the lower level of the building. I had never been to the basement of a hospital before, let alone the morgue. I can still remember the signs hanging from the ceiling and the signage on the walls with arrows routing visitors in the right direction. I didn't know what to expect, except that it would be quiet, and it was. No nurses running around to emergencies down here, no doctors shouting orders, and no rooms full of sick people waiting to be seen by an emergency physician. It was as if being so close to the dead, that everyone, staff and visitors alike, were expected to be respectfully quiet. And they were.

Caroline had changed her mind, she said, she didn't think she could cope, didn't want to go any further, but would I go instead? The words kept running through my mind: I don't want to do this, I don't want to be here and I don't want to go in there. Someone held my elbow and propelled me forward through the doors, leaving my sisters

27

behind on the other side. It was impossible to know what to expect, as the whole situation was surreal to begin with. The police officer and security guard walked with me down a short hall and through another door. There was a man standing there waiting for us; security must have called ahead to let them know we were coming. I'm not sure who he was -- an attendant? A doctor? Who he was didn't really matter, he wasn't what I was focusing on. Instead I was looking at the steel gurney in front of me. And on it there was a black body bag with a seal attached to its zipper. The first thing that went through my mind was how is Dad supposed to breathe in that? And then as I was moved forward, I thought, should I even be this close? Didn't people view bodies through a window or some sort of partition? The police officer broke the seal on the bag and the other man undid the zipper, loudly. No, Dad, no. Why did that zipper make so much noise when he was undoing it? It sounded like rolling thunder and it was deafening me.

He continued to undo the zipper stopping halfway. Oh, no, Dad, oh, no. The horror of what I was seeing in front of me registered slowly. This cannot be my father, there was no way. His face, oh my God, his face. It was gone, churned into a bloodied pulpy mess. The few facial features that remained weren't where they were supposed to be. His nose was flattened and was down closer to his mouth, or what was left of his mouth. The flesh that was still there had nothing to support it, his whole jaw was collapsed. There was a white plastic thing in his mouth that must have been put there to keep the rest of his face from caving in. But your eyes, oh, Dad, your eyes, they were the worst. The left one was swollen shut, but at least it was in the right location on your face. But your right eye, your eye! It shouldn't be down by the bottom of your nose, but it was. Pushed down by the flattened bloody mess that used to be your nose, there was your right eye, open yet seeing nothing.

There wasn't anything on my father's face that I could identify him by except for the one green eye and some of the very top of his forehead that was left. There wasn't any part of his face, neck, throat, or chest that was flesh coloured anymore, it was all bloodied. His right arm was hacked at the elbow, still attached, but barely.

I'm here now, Dad, one of us is here. I want to reach out to you, so you can feel the warmth of my touch, so you know that you aren't alone, that one of us made it to you. I want you to feel that connection, even though there is no life in you anymore, but part of you would know, on some other plane, some other level of existence, you would know that I am here. Of this I am sure. I reach my hand out to touch you, but the police officer tells me not to, that you are evidence now.

Evidence?

You aren't to me though; you are still my Dad.

I tell them I've seen enough and I turn to

leave. My Aunt is behind me, how did she get here? She must have come in with me and I didn't realize it. How did that happen? I must have been shut away in my own mind, unaware of others, seeing only what was in front of me. I am dry eyed, but reeling from what I've just seen. My sisters are on the other side of the second door, waiting. I want to tell them that it wasn't him, I want to tell them that there's been a mistake; but I can't tell them what they want to hear, and I can't say what I wish I could. "I want to see Dad," Caroline says. I take her by the arm, roughly, and move her towards the exit and tell her emphatically that no, she does not, but she continues on. I shout at her "YOU DO NOT WANT TO SEE WHAT I JUST SAW" and tell her that Dad would never ever want any of us to see him like that.

She didn't argue anymore, and we left.

I wasn't sure if I would sleep that night; not sure if I even wanted to. And if sleep were to come, what horrific scene would play out in my mind? I wanted to stay awake forever and try to ward off what I could. I was exhausted, though, completely drained. But sleep would come, fitfully, and it would come in broken pieces. I wouldn't dream of the horror I saw in the morgue, I did not see my father's battered body.

What haunted me that night and would for many more nights to come would be the sound of that zipper.

And now there came both mist and snow,
And it grew wondrous cold:
And ice, most high, came floating by,
As green as emerald.
And through the drifts the snowy drifts
Did send a dismal sheen:
No shapes of man nor beasts we ken
The ice was all between.

The Rime of the Ancient Mariner

Chapter 4 ~ Setting Sail

My Dad was a well-liked man, and between him and my mother it seemed that everyone knew them, or knew of them. Dad worked for many years at PK Welding as a sheet metal worker and machinist and then at Oshawa Sulky. In later years, he also did a lot of work for the City of Oshawa, so he was a familiar face around town as was my mother. Shortly after moving to Ontario she was hired as the payroll clerk for Morris Kohen, of Kohen Box Ltd, and then went on to manage the Queen's Hotel for him until the land was expropriated by the City of Oshawa in the early 1990s. So there was a long list of people who we needed to contact, to reach out to and break the news to.

When I think of my Dad, he would be happy to know that usually the first images of him that come to mind are of when he was still alive, and not the horrific ones of when I last saw his badly beaten body at the morgue that awful night at the hospital. My Dad was a consummate inventor; my lasting memories are of him rushing out of the garage at the house on Gladstone to show us his latest gadget, something that he assured us was guaranteed to make us overnight millionaires. Somehow, despite all his work and all his enthusiasm, it just never happened. It was the promise of something big to come, the possibility of hitting the big time, that propelled him to keep on trying. Plus it was in his genes; he was a born inventor just as his father was before him. Going through my Dad's things after his death, I came across many drawings and patent applications that his father did. Lots of different schematics and sketches to modify farming equipment to make it more efficient. Both my Dad and Grandfather were good thinkers and able to translate their ideas and make something practical out of them with their hands. This is something that I have never been able to do: visualize the end result of something and then sit down and make something with my hands. When I think of my Dad, I remember the quiet man with a good sense of humour and a person who could always fix anything that was put before him. Dad coming out of the garage with visions of the latest need-to-have product that he invented kind of lost its effect on us kids, but not to him; he was always tinkering about with something.

What was never up for debate was his artistic skill and eye for detail. Dad was a proud Navy man, and he spent hours, days, weeks, whatever time it took to precisely build replicas of the ships he had sailed on. Anything that he could find that was to do with the sea, anything, he could make something out of it. He could construct ships in bottles, build replica ships just by looking at pictures of them, right down to the finest detail. And then there was the classic lobster claw ashtray that he made. As years went by I thought I imagined it, and it wasn't until my sister showed me a picture of Dad, Grandma and me that I saw it again. I almost didn't see it either; I was looking at my young self in the photo, with my head tossed back and laughing, holding a blonde doll in my arms. And there was Dad and Grandma, too, just as I remembered them, and then in the forefront of the photo, I saw the famous lobster claw ashtray Dad made -- I couldn't believe it actually existed! But anything that had to do with the sea or the creatures that lived in it, Dad could fashion something from it, nothing would be wasted. Even if claws from a lobster found new life as the decorative part of an ashtray, so be it. And just like the ashtray, I couldn't stop looking at the people in the photo either; I couldn't believe that these people existed once upon a happy time too.

As daughters of a sea-faring father, I look back now and shake my head at some of the normal-to-us but likely crazy-to-other-people life we had. I am the only person I know who has been legitimately traumatized by seafood as I was coaxed, cajoled, and bribed into trying whatever Dad would bring home from the Fish Store. Go on, Lisie, just one bite, just try it, you might like it, he would say as he opened a mussel for me to eat. (I didn't.) Kelp, try some, Dad would say, it'll put hair on your chest. Why this didn't stop me right then and there in my tracks, I don't know, but try some I would. In his mind, there was no point telling me it was dried seaweed until after I tried a bit (too salty). But the beginning of the end of my seafood ventures happened one day after school. I just got in the door and Dad said, hey, Lisie, watch out in the bathroom, just be careful. I looked in, only to find two lobsters crawling around in the bathtub. But that was it, that was the beginning of my traumatization by seafood. To this day I don't eat any; not even the humble tuna sandwich will make it past my lips.

My Dad joined the Royal Canadian Navy in 1949 when he was 17 years old and stayed until 1956. He worked in the boiler rooms of the ships as a stationary engineer and sailed on the HMCS Labrador, Wallaceburg, La Hulloise and Ontario. And I wouldn't be far wrong in saying that they were likely the best days of his life. Not only did his Navy days give him experiences of a lifetime, but it was then that he was also christened with the nickname of 'Slinger' which was what he was almost exclusively called and he referred to himself as. It was, of course, taken from his last name of Slingerland. When growing up, my sisters and I were regaled with stories from his Navy days -- no fairy tale stories for his girls -- and most of them started off with "When your Uncle Bert and I were in the Navy....' I think Dad and my Uncle Bert were legends in their own minds long before any of us realized that they truly were legends. And all of the fantastic travels and things they did together really did seem like tall tales, but they were all true.

My Uncle Bert Duford was not only one of my Dad's best friends, but by marrying sisters they were brothers-in-law as well. They travelled on the icebreaker the HMCS Labrador together which set sail in July of 1954 from Halifax bound for the Labrador Sea. Through the summer, the Labrador and her crew worked their way through Canada's Arctic Archipelago from east to west conducting hydrographic sounding, resupplying RCMP outposts, and deploying assorted scientific and geological teams for research. The Labrador became the first large vessel to transit the Northwest Passage. And then by sailing down the west coast of the United States and through the Panama Canal and then back to Halifax, the Labrador became the first ship to circumnavigate North America in a single voyage. And of that, my father was immensely proud.

Legends? Yes, indeed.

That my Mum and Dad even met up was happenstance as many things in life often are. My mother, Gladys Burke, was born in Charlottetown, Prince Edward Island, and when she was six or seven years old, the family packed up and moved 60 miles away to Pictou, Nova Scotia. The shipyard in Pictou was booming at the time and, like many other families, they went to where the jobs were. Her mother's family, the Johnsons, were all from Halifax, Nova Scotia. Interestingly, long before my mother was born, Halifax played a huge part in our family history. The morning of December 6, 1917,

36

dawned bright and still; it was cold but with little snow on the ground. The routines of the day for the people of Halifax were in motion -- workers were already at their labouring jobs for the better part of an hour, shops were getting ready to open. Businessmen were making their way to offices in the high street, and school-aged children were just beginning their lessons for the day. There was no sense of urgency to the day, no time for anyone, if they knew what was coming, to have one last chance to say good-bye. Shortly after 9am, a French cargo ship, the SS Mont Blanc, was making its way through the Narrows, the strait connecting the upper part of Halifax Harbour to Bedford Basin. The ship, loaded down with wartime explosives, collided with the relief ship, the SS Imo. A fire on the Mont Blanc ignited its cargo and that caused a catastrophic explosion that devastated the Richmond District of Halifax. About 20 minutes after the explosion on the French ship, the second ship exploded. The ship was completely blown apart, with the blast wave travelling at more than 1,000 metres. White-hot shards of iron rained down upon Halifax and Dartmouth, and an area over 160 hectares (400 acres) was totally destroyed by the explosion. It was so huge the harbour floor was momentarily exposed by the volume of water that was vapourized. The blast was the largest man-made explosion prior to the development of nuclear weapons. Nearly all structures within a half-mile radius, including the community of Richmond, were completely obliterated. Over 1,600 people were killed instantly and 9,000 injured, more than 300 of whom later died. Hundreds of people who had been watching the fire from their homes were blinded when the blast wave shattered the very windows they were looking out from. The city was on fire – stoves and lamps overturned in the blast soon set the city alight.

All this was bad enough, and looking back to almost a hundred years in the past, I cannot even imagine the devastation felt by the city of Halifax and her people. And some of those people were my people as they were part of my maternal grandmother, my Nana Madeline Johnson's family. Her father, William Johnson, 40, was a walking supervisor on the docks at the harbour that early December morning. With the explosion of the second ship, my great-grandfather was thrown into the water and, as the family story goes, had worn the skin of his finger tips down trying to claw his way back up onto the wharf to try to save himself before he drowned. Not only did he perish in the Halifax Explosion, so did his 24-year-old second wife Elnora, his son William Junior, aged 15, and baby daughter Mary, 4 months. My Nana Madeline was just starting her school day when the explosion happened, and the children who did not have a clear path to get out of the school by the staircase had to find another way out. Along with her classmates, my Nana leapt from a damaged and burning building to save herself -- by jumping into the coats held open by the sailors on the ground who were shouting to the children to jump. So within a blink of an eye, life for my then-nine-year-old Nana forever changed. Her father, stepmother, brother and baby sister were forever gone; her older brother Art and sister Francis and a few relatives on Prince Edward Island were all she had left. A footnote to this terrible family tragedy is that Art had to identify his brother's remains and only could do so by the pocket watch found on him that day. Two days after the explosion that wiped out Halifax, Madeline Johnson would turn 10 years old, and in the years to come she would speak very rarely of the disaster and the day of terror and devastating loss she and the people of Halifax endured. The loss of the Johnson family became a tragic footnote in our family history, but my Nana was traumatized for the remainder of her life, and I remember her often panicking, thinking that she still had shards of glass in her throat from that awful day. Madeline Johnson Burke died of throat cancer in 1982; she was the last one of William Johnson's family who survived that horrific December day in Halifax in 1917.

Forty years after the devastation that tore apart our family in the Explosion of 1917, Halifax Harbour would come to play a part in our family history once more but this time as a backdrop to a happier story. My Dad was a sailor on the HMCS Wallaceburg and it set down anchor in Pictou, Nova Scotia, where my mother was working part time at Minnie Pentz's palatial Harbourview Inn, doing every odd job imaginable. My Dad and two other sailors came in looking for rooms to rent, as the Wallaceburg was being refitted and they needed a place to stay. When the ship refitting was finished, my Dad sailed away, and when he returned, he was loaded down with presents for everyone and met up with my mother again. The rest, as they say, is history. They stayed in Nova Scotia for a while, and then my Mum decided to follow her older sister Jean and her husband Howard to Ontario. At the time, Dad was working with the Stewart family in Pictou, helping out at their sawmill but made a last minute decision and jumped into the car and headed west to Ontario with everyone. Mum and my Nana moved into an apartment on Ontario Street in Oshawa; and way up in one of the bigger rooms on the third floor that was for rent, who but my Dad would move in. Dad, my Mum said, would always seem to end up with her family somewhere and that he just always seemed to be around. They would later marry and move to an apartment on Richmond Street, just behind the Queen's Hotel. Their next move would be to Gladstone Avenue, where they would raise the three daughters born to them between 1961 and 1969.

Even though my mother's family of Irish settlers were from down East, my Dad was from Ontario and his family lived just across Lake Ontario in the picturesque town of Niagara-on-the-Lake where his mother's family, the Staines from Lincolnshire, England, emigrated from many years before. They could not have chosen a better place to settle, these English relatives of mine. Niagara is located on the western bank of the Niagara River in the Golden Horseshoe area of Southern Ontario, known not only for the world famous landmark of Niagara Falls, but as well for its natural beauty, wineries, and the Green belt. My Dad was born not far away in the city of St. Catharines but grew up in Niagara-on-the-Lake into the deeply rooted United Empire Loyalist Slingerland family of Niagara, whose family ancestral line can be traced back to hundreds of years in the area. Going to Niagara is something I try to do as often as I can, and it always brings back good memories and feels like going home when I do; how can it not, with the strong family history and connections we have there? Mixed in with memories of visiting Grandma Slingerland at the family home on Mary Street, where my sisters and I would pick fresh pears from the trees that grew in her yard, are the memories of the mighty Niagara. Dad would tell us of his adventures of ice fishing on the frozen Niagara River and stories of how he and his sisters would swim across the river to Niagara Falls, New York, in their younger days. Words alone cannot do justice to the splendour of Niagara Falls. The Falls are a sight to behold in any season – whether you see them in the frigid depth of an Ontario winter with plunging temperatures that freeze the fast flowing waterfall into gigantic boulders at the foot of them, or walk towards the brink of the Falls at Table Rock in the

41

height of the summertime, weaving through the never-ending stream of tourists, the heat tempered somewhat the closer you get to the thunderous Falls by their cool mist clinging to you. Niagara and the astounding beauty of the area truly are one of Southern Ontario's gems.

Chapter 5 ~ Breaking Stress

This book is not impossible to write, but it is hard at times to try to find the right words to convey the parts of this story that need to be told. The first few days after receiving the horrible news at the police station became a blur of activity, disbelief and confusion. There were phone calls still to make and people to break the news to and to try to offer what comfort we could. Going to work was out of the question, of course, and all the normal routines of life were put on hold. I called my friends and told them what had happened, and I was grateful for the offers of support they showed me. There was intense media interest as well; my Dad was well known in the Oshawa area, and his murder was to be one of six murders in Durham Region that occurred in the first half of 1991. As a family, we gave no comment to the press, and we bristled when we read things in the papers that weren't completely factual. Both Deb and I at one point worked at the local paper, and it was hard to see our family's grief and our Dad's murder on the front pages of it. People from the area who were interviewed about their reaction to my Dad's death described him as: a smart, quiet, mild-mannered nice man, who had a great sense of humour, and would do anything for anyone.

The police investigation, of course, was still

ongoing. Deb and I would meet at the downtown police station with Detective MacDonald and he tried to keep us abreast of what was happening during the investigation into the murder of our father. He was our direct link to everything; there was no liaison officer back then to help the family, no Victim Support Services that work in the capacity that they do today. So it fell to him to try to help us to find answers to our never-ending questions, to help us fill in the gaps.

The house on Brock Street was no longer sealed as a crime scene, and we were informed that, if we wanted to, we could enter the house and retrieve any personal belongings of our father's. This was a difficult decision and one that Deb and I struggled to make. Yes, we wanted whatever property belonged to our Dad that was in that house. But who knew what horrors we would see when we went inside? The decision was not made lightly; though very apprehensive about it, we decided that we would go to the house together, get what we wanted and then get out again.

At one time, the house was a grand property, one of many well-built, solid and sturdy brick houses in the area. In the heyday of General Motors, in which Oshawa was the car making capital of Canada, these houses were family homes, ideally close to GM and other amenities. However, in the decades since, the area saw a decline and in the late 1980s into the '90s, a lot of the houses that were once family homes were bought cheaply and turned into rooming or boarding houses. One of my Dad's friends was the owner of a few of these houses on the street, and that is how it came to be that Dad was in that area at all. He was a maintenance worker and looked after the repairs of at least three of the houses in the same neighbourhood. At the time of my father's murder, the owner of the house was away in Florida, taking a break from our Canadian winter.

Looking back, out of everything we did, from every decision we made from that time in our lives, this is the one that haunted us both. To find the right words to convey the horrors we saw at the house on that cold day in February seems an impossible task. We made our way up the steps of the porch and tentatively knocked on the front door. A man who was living in the house answered, we explained who we were and he let us in. This house may be a crime scene to us, but this was a rooming house with tenants, and this was their home. Police had given them the okay to return, likely the same time we were told we were allowed into the house if we wanted to retrieve things.

Everything looked in order as we walked down the hallway until we got closer to the room at the back of the house where the altercation started. The violence of my Dad's death were just words to Deborah at that point, but with me seeing my Dad's body at the morgue I had already known how bad the attack was. Nothing, however, could prepare either of us for what we would see in that room.

45

The acrid, coppery smell of dried blood emitted strongly from the room as we moved along the hallway towards it. When we opened the door, the rusty and metallic smelling air hit us like an assault. We turned on the light, illuminating the small room, and as we looked around, we could see blood splatter arced high up the walls, lots of blood with bits of matter mixed in with it. Blood seemed to be on every surface -- on the walls, on overturned furniture, in pools on the carpet, and we could see where portions of the carpet had been carefully removed, cut out for what we could only suppose was evidence. The walls and door frames bore specks of blood and the black marks of the dusting equipment that was left behind by the Forensics team. Deb and I were very quiet as we moved through the room picking up whatever belongings that we recognized as Dad's. We ran some hot water in the sink in the communal kitchen, found some towels, and we both tried to clean the blood off the walls, but to no avail; it was too much of a task for us to take on. I don't even know why it was so important to us to try to clean things up in the first place. Maybe, we thought, as it was part of our Dad, that we could get it off the walls and, by doing so, we could preserve some of his dignity. I can remember my sister crying as she scrubbed at the walls in vain, but there were no tears from me, not then. I was angry. No, angry was too tame of a word, I was furious. My Dad was killed in the early evening; surely there were people in the house who could have come to his aid? There must have been one hell of a fight, and as there was heavy furniture overturned in the room, someone must have heard something. I saw a chain saw I recognized as my Dad's in the corner of the room. I grabbed it, left my sister behind and made my way up the stairs to the rooms that the tenants of the house lived in. I banged on their doors, and tried to keep my emotions in check as I demanded answers from those who opened them to me. Were you home when this happened? Did you hear anything? If you did, did you try to do anything, try to help my Dad? If not, why not? I was looking for answers that I was never going to find, and, of course, the police would have already asked all the same questions of these people who lived there. What did they think, these tenants, of this angry young woman going room to room, banging on doors and demanding answers with a chainsaw in her hand for protection? I didn't care what people thought, I just wanted answers. Answers that would help me make sense of this and would stop the repetitive question of why, why, why that was constantly running through my head.

I went back to the room and Deb had a few things she wanted to take -- tools, odd books and bits and pieces. As she carried them outside to her car, I went over to the sliding glass door that led to a patio and then onto the backyard. There was a lot of black dusting powder on the door frame and handles as well as congealed blood on the sliding track at the bottom of the door, and then even more blood on the other side of it. Looking beyond the door and onto the patio, I could see crimson pools everywhere. Though I didn't know it at this point, this sliding door was where John Terrance Porter dragged my dying father through to finish killing him. I would come to find out later that Porter was interrupted twice by a roomer in the house who came to see what all the shouting and screaming was about that evening. Rather than give up, take off and leave my Dad alone, Porter continued his savage attack. Maybe my Dad would have survived the injuries received at this stage of the assault. But we will never know because, instead of showing a dying man some mercy, John Terrance Porter dragged my Dad through these sliding glass doors and continued to butcher him during a frenzied attack on the patio and in the backyard, all while my father pleaded for his life.

A few days after the visit to the house, I stopped by the fish store to see my Dad's friends. I had updates to share with them from the police, and it wasn't just our family in shock at all that happened -- Dad's friends were having trouble coping as well. The fish store's proper name was Fundy Sea Foods and was owned by a man named Bev Parker. He and my Dad became good friends and his shop was always a popular gathering place for people, and more often than not, you would find my Dad there, either upstairs in the store selling seafood, or downstairs in the basement that he jokingly referred to as his office.

I walked into a store full of customers and friends, all talking about the same thing -- my Dad's murder. No one could quite believe what had happened and struggled with the reality that their friend Slinger was gone. Not just dead, but killed in a savage attack. Bev saw me and took me downstairs so we could speak privately. I told him about what the police had told Deb and me and what little we knew about the investigation thus far. I gave him details about the upcoming funeral and the gathering that would be happening afterwards at the hall beside our family Church.

As I turned to go back upstairs to the shop, something caught my eye and stopped me in my tracks. My Dad's white smock was hanging on the peg where he had last hung it. It was there waiting for him to put on when he came back to the fish store, but, of course, that would never happen again. The tears that didn't fall at the police station that night, the tears that didn't fall when I saw my Dad at the morgue, and the tears that burned my eyes but didn't fall as we tried in vain to scrub our father's blood off the walls of the room he was killed in fell now. All those bottled-up tears fell that day in the basement of the fish store, and once started, I could not stop them. Seeing the white smock that I used to see my Dad wear unleashed an uncontrollable flood. I tried, but I could not stop crying, and by trying to stem the flow, I was making things worse. I was weeping and sobbing so much I couldn't speak and then I couldn't breathe. Bev led me to a nearby chair, sat me down and let me cry and offered what condolences he could but, in the end, he was crying with me.

Hours gave way to days, days to weeks, and things that previously held a lot of importance in our lives didn't even register any more. There were more immediate things to deal with. We had to finish the plans for the funeral that was set for February 13th at our family Parish of St. Gregory the Great, the same church where my parents were married years before. The visitation would be held at Armstrong Funeral Home, one of the local funeral parlours and where we had held the wake for our Nana years before. Deb and I kept ourselves busy making arrangements, trying to make sure that we had everything covered and making sure that things would be just right.

But something bothered me immensely, something nagged at me, and I couldn't rest until I could think of what I could do about it. It was my father's face. I knew that he would never want anyone to see him like that, and it would of torn him apart to know that I did. I was haunted by what I had seen, and as the day of the funeral drew closer, the dreams became worse. In the most vivid of them, the pallbearers were walking with measured steps, slowly proceeding up the Church aisle, their faces reflecting the seriousness and solemnity of their task. Somehow, though, the coffin tipped and my Dad spilled out and then everyone saw him --

and they would be horrified and screaming. It truly was one of the worst of the nightmares I would have, and I would wake in a cold sweat of panic and terror convinced that it really did happen. So I spoke privately to the funeral director the evening before the funeral and handed him a white folded cloth. If he could put this over my Dad's face for me, I said, I would appreciate it, and taking it from me, he assured me he would do so. What this man didn't say to me was that it was a closed coffin and that it wouldn't matter, and that no one would see him anyway; what he didn't ask me was why I needed this done so badly. What he did do was take the cloth from me, no questions asked and assured me he would do as I requested. To my mind, I reasoned, that wherever Dad was on his way to from this world, to whatever part of creation he would end up in, I didn't want anyone or anything else to see what I had seen. My thinking made perfectly good sense to me. And whatever bit of comfort I could find through this, whatever could give me any peace, I would take it.

There was a constant stream of people coming to the wake, offering condolences to our family and wanting to talk and share with us memories they had of Dad. We brought in one of the ships Dad built and Armstrong's put it on a stand to better display it beside his coffin. It was one of his favourites of the ships he built, and I remember how pleased he was when he finally finished it. He christened his new ship the

'Katherine Mary Jaye' using the combination of the middle names of his three daughters. On his coffin we had placed a framed black-and-white photo of him from his Navy days. In it, he's standing tall and proud with a gigantic iceberg as a backdrop, a huge grin on his face. It is one of my favourite pictures of Dad, which was undoubtedly taken during the best time of his life.

And so, on that freezing February morning, many people gathered into the church to say goodbye to Dad. I was surprised to see members of the Durham Regional Police in attendance, but maybe they were there because of their investigation, or maybe they attended out of respect for our family. Pallbearers were made up from a combination of Dad's lifelong friends and of his smartly dressed nephews in their Air Force uniforms. The red and white flag of St. George was draped on his coffin in honour of the English heritage of which he was so proud.

The Oshawa Naval Veterans Club paid their respects to my father by having a Naval Honour Guard present at the entrance of the Church for the duration of the service. Although Church of England by birth, my Dad was not an overly religious man, but through my mother's Irish heritage, we were all raised Catholic. And, as they say, funerals aren't as much for the deceased as they are for the comfort of the living. My Dad was interred at Thornton Cemetery with a full graveside naval gun salute. We thought about having him buried in his beloved Niagara with the rest of the Slingerland family who have lain there for hundreds of years, but at the time and the depth of our loss, it just made sense to us to keep him close to where we all lived. I would like to think that we did Dad proud on that frigid February day, giving him the best send-off we could while filling the service and wake with the things he held important and that he was so proud of in his life.

Somewhere, I hoped, he was looking down and saying 'Well done, my sons, well done.'

Chapter 6 ~ Slow Ahead

It was very hard to try to form some semblance of a normal life in the weeks and months after my Dad's murder. Obviously we would never be the same again. Deb and I were in touch with Detective MacDonald every few days, and he was always patient with us and always had time for our questions. John Terrance Porter was in a cell at the Whitby Jail for the time being, we were told, and would be there until his trial the following spring. That was something else we knew nothing about: trials, courtrooms, lawyers, crown attorneys. Nothing like that had ever touched our lives before. The good people I worked for at the time paid me for all the time I took off work. I eventually returned to my office job, but it would be a very, very long time before Caroline returned to her accountancy job. Deb, who had found out about her cancer diagnosis just before Dad's murder, was starting her radiation treatments at the cancer hospital in Toronto. Dad was gone, and nothing could change that, but Deborah was still here, and she needed all the support she could get.

There were no more hockey games for me, no more meeting up with friends; that carefree existence of my life seemed to be over. The summer plans to return to England seemed like someone else's dream now. I was sad about it too; I wanted to still be that person, still be that girl who was on top of the world, who could have things happen because she planned them, not have things randomly thrown at her that would lead to things spinning out of control. In a way, not only was I mourning the loss of my father but, in a smaller sense, the loss of myself and my life as I knew it and as our family knew it. My Dad's murder was my transition to adulthood; it forced me to grow up, to make adult decisions, and even though I was in my early 20s at the time, it made me wary of the world and some of the people in it. Things that meant so much to me mere months before just didn't seem important anymore. I drifted from the close circle of friends that I had, but it wasn't anyone's fault. We were still on good terms, but things had changed: I had changed. I had different priorities, different things on my mind, things that hopefully my friends would never have to experience. I just felt a huge disconnect from everyone.

But not from my sister Deb. She and I were always close, despite our seven-year age difference. She was not only my big sister; she was the best friend I ever had and the biggest influence in my life. She even named me, and as the family story goes, in the months leading up to me being born, she wasn't interested in having a new brother or sister in her life. After all, she had already had our parents to herself for seven years; she certainly didn't want any new baby infringing on her territory. My mother thought that she would call me

Sarah, naming me after her own Aunt, but to smooth the way for me and probably buy herself a bit of peace, she gave in and let Deb choose a name for me. So, instead of the lovely name of Sarah, I was named after a character from my sister's favourite television show at the time, the American sitcom called 'Green Acres.' Lisa Douglas was played by Eva Gabor and, needless to say, I was driven mad through the years by a teasing older sister singing the show's theme song, 'Green Acres is the place to be!' But by letting her firstborn daughter name her new baby after a fictional television character so to better ease my entrance into this life, my mother did a very wise thing -- she set the cast for an unbreakable bond between my older sister and me.

Our Dad's murder became the elephant in the room for my family: It was there, it touched us all, but it was rarely spoken of. It wasn't just one elephant, though; it was a whole herd of them. This wasn't true for Deb and me -- we talked about things all the time and we relied on one another for almost everything. We would go over the information that Detective MacDonald gave us, we would wonder about the man who killed our Dad, and we would talk about the upcoming trial. Everyone else seemed to retreat into their own private rooms of grief, my Mum and Caroline especially. Perhaps for my mother, she was just repeating the behaviour of her mother and how she dealt with the tragedy that befell her family in

Halifax all those years before. Her mother never spoke about that either.

So life moved on. Priorities changed and dreams were put on hold. There would be no happy return to England for me as I had planned and saved for. I would get back there eventually, but it wouldn't happen for years. There were just too many things to cope with here, too many things happening to even think about leaving. And I would still think the same way after the trial was finished. I couldn't go anywhere; the world had changed for me. I was worried about everyone around me and how they were coping, but I hardly knew a thing about taking care of myself. During the time between the murder and the trial, I struggled. I expected to have bad dreams at night, but in the day, I could be busy with something and then the same thought would hit me from out of nowhere -- Dad wasn't coming back, he was dead, murdered, and not returning to us. Then I would make deals in my mind, broker impossible deals with God. I would take him back, no questions asked, and not only that, but I would take him back despite any injuries he might have. Just give him back to us. No matter what disfigurations or disabilities he would now have, I would take him and take care of him. I could deal with that better than I could deal with this. This thought would catch me unawares, sneaking into my mind when I least expected it; and it was so real, a physical ache so real I could actually feel it, and I would have to sit down because the emotions behind it were so strong.

Just give him back.

We were still in regular contact with Detective MacDonald, and we still asked for updates and information, but there was one other thing that came before all of that: Deb's health and the treatment for the cancer she was battling. Mum and whatever sister was available would go with Deb to Sunnybrook for her cancer treatments, to keep her company and to give her support. Getting her well was our number one priority. Deborah battled the cancer hard, and after the surgery and the radiation that followed, they told her good news -- she had beat it. It had worn her out and wrung all of us out, but she did it, she was cancer free. She would still have to go for regular check ups, but things, for a change, were looking positive.

We met the lead prosecutor for the case of Regina vs John Terrance Porter a few months before the trial. He was a young man named Greg O'Driscoll, and he was part of the Crown Attorney's office for Durham Region. He, along with Detective MacDonald, would help guide us both through the daunting experience of a murder trial. If my sister and I were the faces of the family, they, to us, along with another prosecutor by the name of Randy Evans, were the faces of getting things right and hopefully sending this man away for a long, long time. We spent a lot of time in Greg's office during those months, as he kept us well informed and updated. There didn't seem to be victim support services, depth of information or resources that are made available to people who would be going through something like this now. So Greg and Detective MacDonald were it for us, and looking back, we could not have asked for two better people to help us during this overwhelming time. They both genuinely had our best interests at heart, kept us informed as best they could, and treated us with respect, patience and courtesy.

So when John Terrance Porter was taken from his cell at the Whitby Jail in April of 1992 to the courthouse in Whitby for his trial to face the charge of first degree murder in the death of Roland Lloyd Slingerland, Deborah and I were there for our Dad. It was important to us both, we needed to see this out and hopefully see justice served. We knew that nothing would bring our Dad back. Perhaps, though, the trial would serve as some sort of closure to us, and then we could adjust to the new normal that was now our lives.

Not that it wasn't important for other family members to be there, it was important to everyone, but it was Deb and I who went every day to court for the trial. We were still looking for answers as there were a lot of blanks that needed to be filled in. We had some information, though. The man who killed our Dad was a 31-year-old drifter from the East Coast. His name was John Terrance Porter, but he went by the name of Terry Porter. We found out that he was the adopted son of a New Brunswick police officer, and we also knew from speaking with

Detective MacDonald and Greg O'Driscoll that he was looking for his girlfriend at the house the evening he killed our Dad. We also knew that Terry Porter was found two-and-a-half hours after he killed our Dad, asleep in his car, and covered in blood. He was arrested without incident. His mug shot from that night showed a defiant and disheveled young man. He was to turn 32 years old the next day, one day after he butchered my father.

The trial that had been looming like a black cloud above us began in April 1992, fourteen months after the murder of our father, and would last until the end of June, almost two-and-a-half months. We were anxious for it to begin and hopeful that justice would prevail So I could attend every day, I took a leave of absence from my job, as did Deborah. And she and I were in the courtroom that morning when they chose the five women and seven men who would ultimately decide the fate of Terry Porter.

The presiding Judge at the trial was Justice Sam Murphy. Terry Porter's defense attorneys were Tony Bryant and Del Doucette. Tony Bryant would later go on to defend Paul Bernardo, the infamous school girl killer from St. Catharines and who was also the notorious Scarborough Rapist. We sat and listened and heard that through his defense attorneys, Terry Porter admitted to killing our Dad but should be excused by reason of 'a mental disorder.' However, the prosecution lawyers Greg O'Driscoll and Randy Evans countered this and were trying to prove that Terry Porter deliberately killed Mr. Slingerland on February 5th of 1991.

Pathologist Doctor David McAuliffe from the Coroner's Office in Toronto took the stand to describe for the courtroom the injuries sustained by my father. Dr. McAuliffe estimated that the right arm of Mr. Slingerland was eighty percent severed at the elbow, probably by a hatchet-type instrument. He then went on to say that the major cut to his right arm and massive injuries to the upper body and head of the 58-year-old man were the cause of death. I didn't have to think too long why my Dad's right arm was almost hacked off, he was likely holding it above him trying to shield himself from the axe or hatchet that Terry Porter was swinging at him. The autopsy conducted two days after his death showed Mr. Slingerland's injuries included a massive fracture of facial bones and to the jaw and to the base of the skull. He also suffered two stab wounds to the chest, a deep, long cut to the right side of the jaw, as well as numerous bruises and cuts. Facial injuries, he continued, on Mr. Slingerland also included a fractured mouth, a fractured nose, and a fractured pharynx. The pharynx was, he explained, the tube that, along with its surrounding membrane and muscles, connects the mouth and nasal passages with the esophagus. There was also a small amount of subarachnoid hemorrhage, bleeding in the area between the brain and the thin tissues that cover it.

There was also a massive rupture of the right

lobe of his liver. Dr McAuliffe also stated that my Dad's liver was probably ruptured and his ribs broken when his attacker stomped on his chest. There were fractures of the right ribs 2-8 anterior, 2 3 4 5 6 AL 9, 10 AL and 7th posterolateral; on the left side ribs 2 3 4 5 6 7 8 anterolateral and 8 9 10 11 lateral. I might add, and this can be taken as an accurate measurement of Terry Porter's rage that evening, he stomped so hard on my father during his brutal attack that he left the impression of his bootprint on my Dad's chest.

In conclusion, he testified that his findings were massive blunt force trauma and chopping injuries with major skull and facial fractures, massive chest injuries, collapse of the lungs, rupture of the liver, subarachnoid hemorrhage and a stab wound to the lung. Cause of death would be documented as massive blunt force and chopping injuries.

Our poor Dad.

I'm not sure if Deb and I had even one decent night of sleep throughout the trial. We learned that the majority of the blows that killed our Dad were inflicted in the house and the remaining outside. Greg O'Driscoll and Detective MacDonald were good to us, though, and would warn us what was coming up that day in court or the next day, giving us ample time to decide if we wanted to leave the courtroom. So when it came time for the Identification Officer to take the stand to show the jury charts and photographs of our Dad's body and the crime scene, we had a choice. We could stay and put ourselves through that, or we could leave. We decided instead of hearing and seeing these graphic details, we would sit outside in the hallway. I had already seen my Dad in the morgue, and she and I both had seen the blood splatter on the walls ourselves, and that was enough for us.

There was a young man at the trial whose testimony has stayed with me all these years. When Deb and I were trying to clean up our Dad's blood at the crime scene, I remember asking her where was everyone? Did no one hear what was going on? Surely there must have been shouting and screaming as Dad was being attacked. Why didn't someone come and help him? It was at that time when I grabbed the chainsaw and went door to door demanding answers from the tenants who were in. During the trial, we learned that, in fact, there were people home and who came to aid my Dad as best as they could. A young man named Matthew testified that the man whom he identified as Terry Porter said something like "it doesn't concern you, it's none of your business" when Matthew came into the room to see what was going on. As he walked back to his room on the third floor, he heard the man asking my Dad: "Where is she? Where is she?" A short while later, Matthew returned again only to see my Dad sitting on the room's floor with "Terry Porter standing over him with his back to the doorway. He turned around and we made eye contact." At that point, Matthew said, Porter told

63

him to mind his own business. "It sounded like he meant business so I left. I was scared." Another tenant who checked to see what was going on went back to Matthew's room and told him that "something's going on downstairs." While Matthew called the police, the other tenant went outside to get the license plate number of Terry Porter's car. They went back to the room to check on my Dad, but he wasn't there; he was now lying down outside on the patio.

Greg O'Driscoll told the jury that they didn't have to worry about "who did it" but what Porter's state of mind was that night. He said that evidence at the trial would show Porter lived with a woman at the rooming house on Brock Street East for about a month around November of 1990. While Porter was away from the house for about an hour, the woman moved out without telling Porter where she moved. He told the court that evidence would show that Porter returned to the Brock Street house to find her on February 5.

The man who owned the houses that were being rented, and who took my Dad on as a maintenance man, was also a long-time friend of my father's. It was his turn now to take the witness stand. He told the hushed courtroom that it was he who helped to move the woman to his daughter's house and later to another home in Uxbridge after the woman confided to his wife the day before that Porter had beat her. When Porter returned to the house, he became frantic when he discovered that she was missing. Porter asked him where she was, and the owner of the house said that he didn't know.

Deb and I loosely knew this information already, with Greg sharing what he could with us during the time we spent together in his office. But to be in the courtroom and to listen to the man who owned the house tell how he moved this woman away – not once but twice! – was absolutely surreal. Here was the reason for Dad's murder. I couldn't speak for my sister, but I know what was going through my mind, and what has always gone through my mind: Terry Porter got the wrong man. My Dad had nothing to do with anything. He didn't move anyone. He didn't spirit anyone away. Dad was telling Terry Porter the truth; when this savage, brutal man demanded of him, "Where is she? Where is she?" he didn't know where she was.

Oh, Dad, it wasn't supposed to be you.

So now we had some answers as to the why part of the murder. Terry Porter was a jealous man who came to town looking for his girlfriend. And Terry Porter's former girlfriend was the next person to take the stand. She testified that he was jealous and abusive towards her. She said Terry Porter seriously hurt her about ten times and rarely let her out of his sight during their two-and-a-half year relationship. She said when she left Porter in November of 1990, it was with the help of the owner of a Brock Street rooming house that she and Porter lived in for about three weeks. Over her two days of testimony, she described to the court and jury her life with Terry Porter since they began living together in Medicine Hat, Alberta, in September of 1988. She said they moved briefly to Moncton, New Brunswick, and after that it was mostly continuous travelling across Canada and through the United States, living out of Porter's car. Their longest stay, she continued, was the three weeks which the two of them spent living in the Brock Street rooming house. During this time, neither she or Porter worked; she testified that they "supported themselves solely on the welfare system." "How does someone support themselves on welfare?" my sister whispered to me. The former girlfriend continued to explain how they used a number of phony pretexts, including using false names to obtain welfare assistance in cities across the country.

When Terry Porter's ex-girlfriend was finished testifying at the trial, she was flown back to Alberta to serve her 15-month jail sentence. She was convicted the month before on a number of charges, including welfare fraud.

Whatever Deborah and I thought of her, or what anyone else's opinion of her was, Terry Porter's former girlfriend was the only person out of the many who testified at the trial who approached us after her testimony and sincerely apologized to us for her part in our Dad's murder.

This trial was giving us answers to the factual questions, the who, what, where, and when of things. But it was the why part of the equation that haunted us. Why Dad? Why didn't Terry Porter just leave when that roomer interrupted him? Why did he need to find his girlfriend so badly? There was just one person who could provide the answers we were looking for, and that was Terry Porter himself.

And, unbelievably, he was going to take the witness stand to defend himself and his actions from that night.

He still looked like the defiant, surly man that we had only ever previously seen in a mug shot photo. Medium build, dark hair, and he looked like he could hold his own in any fight. We saw his back every day in the courtroom, of course, sitting at the defense table scribbling away on a notepad. But he never turned around to look at us. Maybe he was told not to. We didn't want him to look at us anyway. And it's not like Deb and I drew attention to ourselves in court either. We weren't the type to be hanging on to each other weeping and crying with every detail that came up. No, we just sat and listened, took it all in, and then would go over it during the lunch break and then again later at home. Surely, we thought, he would have been advised by his counsel not to take the stand? Maybe he was so full of himself that he thought he could bluff his way through anything, maybe he already had a lot of practice through his life. As much as Terry Porter sickened us, as much hatred we had for him, we wanted to hear what he could possibly come up with to defend his actions that night.

We were all ears.

He began his story and told of being adopted and being shocked when he found out about it when he was five or six years old. How he had dropped out of school when he was in grade 7 or 8 and took up drinking and then later drug use on a regular basis as he hit his teens. He told about his arrests and convictions through the years, about his criminal past. We knew from the meetings with Greg that he had an extensive record, including a conviction of trying to kill his own father years before. And it would be many years later that I would find out the full details of that. We heard about his lengthy history of mental problems that dated back to his teen years, the mental problems on which he blamed his actions on the evening of February 5, 1991.

Terry Porter testified that the last thing he remembered before the fatal February 5th beating was drinking and smoking some drugs with an acquaintance at a house. Next thing he knew, he said, was that he was in the back of a police car and someone telling him that he was charged with first degree murder. He also went on to say that he didn't know how he got there.

The following day at the Whitby Jail, where he was being held, Porter said "he couldn't really believe that he had killed someone. I thought it was a set up," he went on, and that "he didn't know what to make of it." Porter said he went to the rooming house earlier in the morning to "ask

Slinger if his girlfriend was around." On the day of the killing, "Slingerland told him that she was around at Christmas but he didn't know where she was." Porter said he spoke with Slingerland for about ten minutes at the house, and then he left.

Porter said he stopped in a few of the hotels in town and the men's hostel before hooking up with a friend, who also said he hadn't seen Porter's girlfriend. While he was there, they drank some beer and smoked some drugs. When the beer ran out, the two men took some empty beer bottles back to the store for a refund, and there they bought a quart of rye and resumed drinking. Terry Porter said he could not remember returning to the Brock Street rooming house at 6 pm.

Very few murders are random attacks and usually victims know their killers. Terry Porter knew my father in the capacity of a landlord; someone who would collect rent, do repairs and odd jobs around the rental house and tend to the property. Porter went on to say that during his and his girlfriend's stay in Oshawa, they both spent most of their time in the local hotels drinking. He said he had very little contact with Mr. Slingerland during that time. Porter admitted hitting his girlfriend once because she became argumentative when she got drunk. " She had hit me first. I hit her.....in the face." Porter said that he was shocked and worried about his girlfriend when she disappeared in November, and he said that he looked for her at a couple of bars that night without any success. The next day, he said, he turned in his key to the hostel and drove to New Brunswick. He then ricocheted across the country, driving to Alberta in December of 1990 where he lived off and on for about two months. Porter said he asked some acquaintances whether they had seen his girlfriend but denied that he was actively searching for her.

Three days before the murder, he said he left Alberta and headed east because the police had been looking for him at the hotel where he had occasionally rented a room. Porter's defense attorney Tony Bryant told the five-woman, seven-man jury that there is no question Porter caused Slingerland's death on February 5th. "What Mr. Porter is challenging" he said, is that he caused the first-degree murder of Roland Slingerland. Bryant told the jury that they "will hear evidence from various doctors which will urge them to come to the conclusion that Porter was suffering from mental illness." It was a good sob story, but Deb and I weren't buying it, and we hoped to God that the jury would have enough sense not to buy it either. There was not one ounce of remorse from Terry Porter during his two days of testimony on the witness stand. Not that we expected there to be: cold and calculating killers rarely are remorseful.

And yes, medical records produced at the murder trial did show that Terry Porter had been admitted and discharged from various psychiatric facilities across Canada eleven times since the age of 17. Lead prosecutor Greg O'Driscoll suggested to him that he had faked his psychiatric symptoms over the years in order to be admitted into psychiatric facilities to do 'easy time' instead of more difficult custodial time in a prison setting. Terry Porter strenuously denied this.

Not only being a fantastic lawyer and all-round good guy, who knew then that Greg O'Driscoll, with that statement about Porter faking things to spend easier time in psych facilities, was able to look twenty years into the future?

So now, almost three months after it began, the trial was winding down and in its final stages. Warm spring days gave way to hot and humid summer ones, and Deb and I had attended every day thus far, with various family members and friends coming with us from time to time. The trial wore both of us out mentally, and as Deb was still rebounding from her cancer treatments, it wore her out physically as well. The defense and crown rested their cases agreeing upon only one thing: that John Terrance Porter did indeed cause the death of 58-year-old Roland Lloyd Slingerland on the evening of Tuesday, February 5th, 1991. That was not debatable. The task of the jury was to decide if John Terrance Porter was suffering a form of mental illness at the time and, therefore, should be excused for his actions. Or, as the Crown put forth, was John Terrance Porter a cold-blooded, violent, remorseless killer who had deliberately killed a man?

Each day we were in court, and as time went on, we were getting answers to the questions that dodged us. It was like fitting pieces of one of those massive jigsaw puzzles together. And that is how I came to think of the prosecution and the defense. Both sides were given a box of the same puzzle, each box having the same amount of pieces. Day by day, they would put the pieces in place, each side trying to make them fit. When they were finished, when both sides had completed their puzzles, they handed it over to the jury to look at. It was then up to the jurors to examine both puzzles and to see which way things fit the best. Did everything fit in the defense's puzzle, or did some pieces not fit right? Maybe the defense lost a few pieces of their puzzle, which left gaps in the picture. Or did the prosecution make it all fit into place? Did the final picture of their puzzle look better, did things just fit right? A verdict would be reached when all the jurors looked at the puzzle the same way. If things didn't fit for the defense, the jurors would come back with a guilty verdict. If the prosecution couldn't make things fit together, the verdict would be innocent. A hung jury would be declared when the jury could not agree on how the puzzle pieces fit.

The jury deliberated for approximately two days before notifying the judge that they had reached a verdict. They unanimously found John Terrance Porter guilty of the first degree murder in the death of Roland Slingerland. Thank God, thank God. Headlines from local and Toronto newspapers of the day read "Drifter gets life for killing Oshawa handyman." The Toronto Sun dubbed Terry Porter the 'Hatchet Killer' in their headline and accompanying article that told of how he would be jailed for life. We, as a family, were elated. Nothing would bring our Dad back, and nothing could erase the wounds that Terry Porter inflicted on us, but the sentence of Life Imprisonment with no parole eligibility for 25 years was a step toward our healing. There were no winners in this, however, not my Dad, not us, not even Terry Porter. I have never had one iota of pity for the man who murdered my father -- he committed a despicable crime and was held accountable for it, and I hoped that his time in jail would be far from an easy one. But I couldn't help thinking that not only did he take my Dad's life, but in doing so, what a colossal waste he made of his own life as well.

A few weeks after the trial was over, I met with Greg O'Driscoll one last time. He gave me a Certificate of Conviction certifying that on the 27th day of June, 1992, at Whitby, the accused, John Terrance Porter was tried upon the charge of first degree murder and was convicted of the said offence and the following punishment was imposed upon him/her, namely, life imprisonment, with no eligibility for parole for 25 years.

I thanked him for all his hard work, for his kindness and support, and said I would keep in touch. I would speak to Greg a few times through the upcoming years, but I wouldn't meet up with him again for another twenty. Deborah would never see him again.

As for Detective Rod MacDonald? We would never be in touch again, but I would think of him so very often in the years to come. I can't even picture what he looks like anymore, but I can still hear his words. On one of my many trips to the police station where he and I would sit down to talk about things, he told me he was going to give me a bit of advice. He said that when everything was over, when the trial was finished, and despite everything I'd seen and everything I'd heard, I wasn't to become bitter. Because if I were to become bitter, he told me, if I let things eat away at me, then I would become another one of Terry Porter's victims.

I will never be a victim, I told him, never.

Goodbye Dad, I will miss you.
Twenty-two years was not long enough to have you in my life and you left so suddenly.
I will never forget you, Dad.

Lisie

Deep blue sea baby deep blue sea
Deep blue sea baby deep blue sea
Deep blue sea baby deep blue sea
It was Willie what got drowned
In the deep blue sea

Dig his grave with a silver spade
Dig his grave with a silver spade
Dig his grave with a silver spade
It was Willie what got drowned
In the deep blue sea

Lower him down with a golden chain
Lower him down with a golden chain
Lower him down with a golden chain
It was Willie what got drowned
In the deep blue sea

Cover his face with a silken veil
Cover his face with a silken veil
Cover his face with a silken veil
It was Willie what got drowned
In the deep blue sea

Golden Sun bring him back to me
Golden Sun bring him back to me
Golden Sun bring him back to me
It was Willie what got drowned
In the deep blue sea

Chapter 7 ~ Adrift

It was very hard to get back into a routine and make life some sort of normal again in the time after my Dad's murder and the end of the trial. Our routine during that spring and summer was going to the courthouse every day; it was something to keep us busy, something to occupy us. There was a void, of course, but going to court filled some of it. At least we felt we were doing something.

And how I wish I could say that it was easy to follow the advice that Detective MacDonald gave me, but it wasn't. I wouldn't let myself be bitter, but I was still angry, so very angry. And all my anger was directed at Terry Porter. I hated him for what he took, hated him for what he damaged in each of us, and hated him for what he would rob us of in the future. He may have left his fingerprints and marks behind at the crime scene, but he also left his mark on us as well. Locked up in a prison cell, his killing days were over, but my family and I would continue to bleed for years to come.

I returned to work, as did Deb. I only did the office job, deciding not to go back to the evening cleaning job I had. I was still in touch with the close circle of friends, but getting together happened less and less. The less I saw of people, the less was required of me to answer their questions. Or worse still, to see people's pity, or to see their sadness. It wasn't that people didn't mean well; they did. And it wasn't that I didn't appreciate everyone's support, but for me, it was easier to try to put things in the past and try to get on with my life. Some of my friends from those long ago days of 'before' would tell me, years later, that sometimes I would talk to them about things, tell them of my grief and sorrow, but I have no recollection of this. It was as if their words in my mind were penciled in, and so very easily rubbed out and erased, as if my mind sifted through everything, decided what to keep and to brush away the rest.

As the years went by, my anger dissipated somewhat. I was still angry about the death of my father and would despair at the senselessness of it, but the feelings would become less intense. Oh, I still wanted nothing but the worst for Terry Porter in whatever prison he was being held at, and I hoped that his existence was a miserable one. But there was something else I never felt before: fear. Intense anger in other people, whether it was directed to me or not, would frighten me; voices raised in anger could strike a fear in me that I hardly even knew existed before. Did I live a sheltered life beforehand? I didn't think so. But with my Dad's murder I had seen firsthand how fast and uncontrollable a rage could burn, then ignite, and how quickly someone's life could be extinguished because of it. I had been exposed to a different side of life that I scarcely knew existed, exposed to a different kind of anger I had never seen before. This was my reality now, and as hard as I tried to move forward, there were memories and flashbacks that would always try to pull me back.

But life moved on. I got married and had my first child, a daughter, six years after my Dad was murdered. It was bittersweet: she would be his second granddaughter, as she had a cousin who was born a year earlier. The old pain lingered on, though, and I would think of how unfair it was that Dad missed out on being a part of his grandchildren's lives. I wondered if the man who moved Terry Porter's girlfriend from the house that wintertime got to meet his grandchildren? I was always comparing things, what his life was like, what he would have a chance to experience because he wasn't at the house that night when Terry Porter came looking for answers, and my thoughts would almost drive me mad in the process. Yes, the anger was still there, but there was something else, too, that would lessen the anger to help ease it. Love for my little girl and watching her grow up, her smiling face, infectious laugh and her fascination for everything new. She and Deb would spend lots of time together too -- playing or outside blowing bubbles and doing arts and crafts. Life wasn't all bad, you see; there was goodness in it as well, I just needed to look for it harder sometimes, I would remind myself. I tried to keep her Grandpa Slinger alive for her, too: I would try to remember the tall tales of his seafaring glory days and share them with her, just as I know he would have if he were still around. I'd drag out the ships in bottles that he made and let her marvel at them and show her what books of his that I had. But about his murder I said very little. When she was very young, she asked me why I had no Daddy, and I said that I did, but he was in Heaven. Why, what happened? Well, a bad man hit him, I told her, and he couldn't get better again. And that was it. Right or wrong, through the years I said nothing else about his death. I'm sure, though, as the years moved on and she grew up, she likely asked her older cousin about it and they would share what information they might have heard. I was glad that she didn't ask me much about things; it would be too hard to answer, and as she got older, I knew 'the bad man hit him' answer wouldn't appease her like it did when she was younger.

But I was struggling, still, years after my Dad's death. I don't know which was worse, the sleeping hours with uncontrollable nightmares, or the waking hours with out-of-control thoughts. To wake up in the morning from the escape of sleep, no matter how fractured it was, to the fuzzy, blurred reality of what happened and of what life had become. And God help me, pulling up the zipper of my coat, or hearing someone zipping up a suitcase could stop me in my tracks and inwardly make me flinch: it was some of the fallout from that evening in the morgue. Now a few years removed from Dad's murder, the paralytic vise of grief was gone, but the emptiness was still there. This was the new normal in our lives, adjusting to the changes of not just who was missing, but what part of ourselves were gone as well. And whoever said that time healed all wounds got it terribly, terribly wrong. Time didn't heal our wounds: what time did was allow to us to gradually, reluctantly, accept the changes in our lives.

My visit to the morgue that night and seeing what Terry Porter did to my father, seeing his handiwork firsthand painted my dreams and nightmares red for a long time. But as the years went by, the nightmares would subside altogether. Instead, they were replaced by a single dream that would visit me just once a year. It was Dad as he used to be, and he was back with us. We would say, Dad! Where were you? Where have you been? He would try to tell us, but then we would just rush around him, our non-stop talking drowning out his words. We were so excited to see him again, and we didn't care where he had been. It didn't matter that he hadn't been in touch for such a long time, we no longer cared that we didn't get a chance to say goodbye to him. We were just happy to have him back. And we took him back, no questions asked. And the dream would end right there. Once a year, the same dream, the same joy, the same ending. And in the early morning hours, before sleep fully evaporated and wakefulness settled in to dispel it, I would lay there and think that it really had happened, that when I opened my eyes, he really would be back. It was a dream, and I was very happy in my mind before I fully woke up, but it was a cruel kind of dream as well. My nightmares of old were based on the reality of what had happened, and this new yearly dream was based on what we could never have: our father back with us.

So we struggled on. Deb and I did the math, looked in the future to the 25-year eligibility mark of Terry Porter's parole date, working out how old we would be, marveling at such high numbers, surprised that we would ever be that old. At his parole date, Terry Porter would be 57, one year younger than my Dad was when he killed him. It didn't seem fair. His life would be beginning again at almost the same age as my father's ended. But it seemed a very long way off, a lifetime away. Surely, we thought, this man would never see the light of day again, that he would never be set free. A life for a life – Dad was no longer with us, so it only seemed right, only seemed fair that Terry Porter would spend the rest of his life in prison. We were good with that, too, and we had the certificate of conviction, a federal document that stated that, and a jury agreed with us. A year after our Dad's death, Deb wrote a letter about her feelings about losing Dad and the savage way he was killed. Someday she hoped she could send it to the Parole Board, someday she'd like to tell Terry Porter exactly what she thought of him.

When I was growing up, my Dad and I spent many evenings outside sitting behind my Godfather

Paul's house, relaxing on the blue bench that my Dad made. My Godparents were an older couple named Paul and Flo Smith, and they were my parents' next-door neighbours who had no children of their own. So when my parents asked them to be my Godparents, they happily accepted, and I have fond memories of them both. The blue bench behind their house became a meeting place for me and Dad, a place we could sit and spend some time together. And there we would be: heads tipped back, our faces upturned while our matching green eyes searched the inky night skies high above us. Dad would look for faces in the sky and connect patterns in the twinkling stars, point them out to me, and I'd be squinting to find them. Suddenly, a streak of light: Did you see it, Lisie? It was a shooting star hurling through the heavens and it was gone before I could really even find it. I wondered aloud what my chances were of seeing another one: "Wind travels," Dad would tell me, "in the direction of the shooting star", and we'd sit and watch, waiting for another as the summer breeze moved gently around us.

It even seems irrelevant to even mention somewhere in this story that my parents were divorced. Irrelevant because to us it was just the way things were, and Dad was always around. And he was around even more when, best of all, he moved in right next door with my godfather! My godmother had passed away and my godfather was in declining health, so my Dad moved in with him to help him out. Remember earlier that my mother said that my Dad just seemed to be everywhere she looked? He really was. And it worked. It might not have worked for other people, but it did for us. Looking back, did my Dad drink too much? Probably. Did this contribute to why he and my mother split up? Likely. But it's not really for me to say, not really my business. All I know is that he was our Dad. He never raised his voice to us, never raised a hand to us. He was a good cook, could make a tasty Sunday roast for supper even if he did have to scrape the Yorkshire puddings off the bottom of the pan. He was a wine maker and had a huge set-up in my godfather's basement. After all, he didn't have to look far for grapes, he would just amble next door to our house and pick them from the vines from Niagara that he transplanted years before! He would play cards with us, teach us how to play darts, and he made the most extravagant walk-in playhouse for Deborah when she was young. (Caroline and I made it ours, too, only because we pushed our way in.) He treated our sister Madelyn from our mother's second marriage very well and, of course, he gave her a nickname too -- he would refer to her as 'sweets.' He was a winter-sock-wearing-with–sandals-on-at-the-same-time kind of Dad, rounding out his look with a plaid shirt. Plaid shirts buttoned up in the wintertime, but undone and blowing in the breeze in the summertime, and a ball cap perched on top of his head that would complete his look. He loved the sea, he loved fishing, he loved Niagara.

And he loved his girls.

The summer before he died, late one evening, Dad and I were out sitting on the blue bench. I had my pictures with me from my solo visit to England the month before and we were going through them. We talked about many things that night, but for whatever reason, there was a change to the conversation. Lisie, he began, "I don't know how someone could take anyone else's life, I don't know how they could live with themselves." I don't remember what preceded this conversation, or what even got us on to this topic to begin with. But what I do know is that my Dad believed in an eye for an eye. One life for another. I didn't have any opinion on the subject, not then. Years later, though, recalling that conversation, I knew what my father's thoughts were on capital punishment, which had been abolished in Canada in 1976. Fifteen short years later, the abolishment of capital punishment in Canada would affect me directly with the murder of my father. But I was satisfied with the life sentence that Terry Porter received and I didn't think that by executing him that it would right the wrong of him killing my dad. So life imprisonment was sufficient for me. Life behind bars was his sentence, where he belonged and where he would stay.

Silly, naive me.

Chapter 8 ~ Between the Devil and the Deep Blue Sea

How do you measure absence? How can you even begin to try? At first, you measure it by days, weeks, and months that somehow turn into years. Then it's measured in events missed -- marriage, birth of a child, and other milestones. You are still happy for the day and joyful at the occasion, but there is a void. There is also an awareness at the same time that something is missing; someone is missing. You then wonder what their reaction to something would be, some life event, and what they would think about other people that you bring into your life. This becomes circular, and over time I didn't even realize that I was doing it, and try as I might, I couldn't stop it. And the cat and mouse game of the 'what-ifs' led me on a merry chase for years and still continues to do so.

I wondered at times about Terry Porter as well. Was he sorry for what he did, for what he took? I wondered if murderers ever think of their victims' families at all. Do they think about the pain they've inflicted and the very physical ache of longing that the families are left with? Do they know anything of how hard it is to try to put things behind them and then try to move on? Or do they even care? It was as though, by the absence of my father in my life, there was a new presence in it and his name was Terry Porter. Seemingly out of nowhere, he descended on us and wreaked havoc on our lives. Through no fault of ours, he was tethered to us now, and who knew when he might descend upon us again. I tried not to think incessantly of him, I tried not to give him that much of my time, but I did wonder. What did his family think? Were they horrified by his actions, or did they always think that his rage would finally get the best of him and that he would end up killing someone? I do remember at one point someone told me at the time of the trial that when his family found out about the senseless killing of my father, they washed their hands of him. I do know there wasn't one person, friend, family or otherwise, who took the witness stand to support him. And I wondered, too, if while in prison, was he co-operative and adhering to whatever prison protocols that were now part of his daily routine? Or was he resistive and abusive to people in the prison system like he'd been in his life outside of prison? After all, he had 32 years of inflicting his abuse and anger on others; how was that going over in prison? Sometimes I found it hard to shut off my questioning mind.

Another thing happened to me in the intervening years. The word murder hardly escaped my lips. If I bumped into someone from my school days, and they just happened to ask how my parents were, I'd say, Oh, Mum is fine, but my Dad passed away years ago. Or he's no longer with us, or simply that he died. If I were to say that he was murdered, that would only prompt questions, and then from there, I would have to go into things that I was no longer willing to easily talk about. And I was very conscientious of shocking people or making them sad, so it was easier just to say he passed away. So it is as if the word 'murder' was taken out of my vocabulary and it was replaced with softer, more acceptable words, words that would sadden people but not horrify them. But, of course, the truth was that Dad didn't just die, pass away or move on to a better place: he was murdered and his life was violently ended by another human being. And this change in my words, this softening of them, happened gradually without me even noticing it, and not even being aware that I didn't say it anymore. In my mind, when turning over things, murder was an ever-present word, but I wouldn't say it out loud. So my dad's murder came to affect everything about me, right down to my vocabulary.

My Dad's murder left me feeling very isolated and very disconnected from everyone else I knew. I didn't know one other person who had lost a parent or a family member to murder. My father's violent death was always with me, dormant under the surface of my being, only resurfacing when I was alone, lost in thought or under a lot of stress. Then the old anger would flare up and people would wonder what had set me off. I knew, of course, but it was too much to go into. And besides, I thought, they probably wouldn't understand anyway. There was a private room in the house of pain and grief that I would gradually retreat into, stepping so silently into it that I wasn't even aware that I opened its door.

At least I had Deborah. Thank God we had each other. Caroline would never be able to talk about Dad again, not even to us. Just speaking about him brought her so much pain, so it was easier for her not to. But not Deb. She was such a huge link to Dad, and she helped keep him alive for me. Remember when this happened, or remember when he said that, she would ask me. She helped to keep the painful memories at bay while we reminisced and laughed as she reminded me about the good ones. Remember when he set up the sleeping bags out back for us to lie on? He had everything set up just so, including his prized hammock, which he had made himself. We were all laying there waiting, and with much fanfare, he laid down on the hammock only to have it split right down the middle and him fall through it! With stories like these between us, we would keep our Dad alive for each other, and we were determined to remember the good before the bad. I did tell Deb the horrors of what I saw in the morgue that night, and it was in her nature and likely her mission to help eradicate it somewhat by keeping positive, happier images of Dad going through my mind. And reflecting back from where I am now, she did a great job. But for our sister Caroline, over the years she would see a revolving door of therapists, grief counselors, and doctors. We would try to reach out to her, but it was as if things cut her deeper and she bled more-- it was almost as if she didn't have the strength or willpower to stop things from hurting her so much.

So we moved on. Deb and I were like glue, often spending the whole day together and then go back to our homes and then be on the phone again with each other only a few hours later. I was married and busy with my little girl, but Deb was still a very important person in my life, in all our lives, to her sisters, and Mum, too, of course. Deb would help with doing things for our mother, painting her house, cutting her grass, or helping with the dreaded wallpaper duties, and she used to jokingly refer to our family as the 'firm' in regards to the amount of work she did for us! But she was one of those people whose outlook on life was that by doing good deeds and by helping others was a way to pay rent for the time she was lucky enough to get here on Earth. Maybe her earlier scare with cancer made her realize what life was really all about, or what it should be all about. And she carried a card in her wallet with a quote on it that meant a lot to her. "I shall pass this way but once, any good that I can do, any kindness that I can show to any man, let me do it now, let me not defer it, let me not neglect it, for I shall not pass this way again." And, really, those were words she lived by, and each month she would set aside a certain amount of money to buy extra groceries and drop them off to the St. Vincent Pallotti's Kitchen, which helped feed the less advantaged. She also had a lot of time for her little nieces, who were then aged 4, 5, and 6. Because of her cancer surgery years before, she couldn't have children of her own, so very special bonds were forged with those three little girls. And, as she watched her nieces grow, she would wonder what our Dad would say to three more girls in the family and not a boy in sight! Those little girls would be his grandchildren, and how sad that they never got to meet him. He would have a whole new set of 'sons' in his life, with all those granddaughters, and as time moved on, he would come to have a set of great-granddaughters as well.

So as the seasons of our lives changed, and as the years moved on, there came a time that we were happy again. We would never forget, never, but we had moved forward as best we could. New routines and new people came into our lives, and little children made our world a happier one. Oh, of course, Terry Porter was still in prison, and that satisfied us: he was in Kingston Penitentiary doing whatever a man facing a life sentence does. We had built new lives for ourselves, built them on the broken foundations of our old lives, mind, but slowly we began to piece our lives back together. We would never forget the trauma and all that we had been through, never forget our loss or completely recover from it, but we did the best we could.

In the years after her surgery for cancer and

the treatment that she received for it, Deb would go to Toronto for routine check-ups, and there was always positive news coming home and such relief in getting the all clear. Six months after she was told that she didn't have to go for check-ups anymore, she went to a walk-in clinic complaining of a chronic pain between her shoulder blades. She felt a sharp pain, she told me, whenever she took a deep breath or coughed. This had been going on for a few weeks, but she didn't have a family doctor. The doctor who had treated her cancer was closing her practice as she was returning to school to further her studies. Deborah was then put on a waiting list for a regular family doctor and, in the meantime, whenever she was unwell, she would have to rely on walk-in clinics. A lot of people did, though; there was a shortage of doctors in Ontario at the time, and walk-in clinics became a way of life for many people.

So Deborah explained to the doctor at the walk-in clinic what was going on. She was coughing, and at times that pain between her shoulder blades would come on again and it would be unbearable. The doctor suggested that she should lose some weight and that should solve her problem. Unreal, who was this doctor, I asked her, some sort of quack? So that's the unfortunate name we would refer to him as from then onwards: Dr. Quack.

A week later, she was at another walk-in clinic; this one was in the building where her doctor used to practice. The pain was getting worse, and our mother had strongly suggested that she go and get checked out again. This time we hoped she might actually get lucky and see a doctor who could just possibly know what they were doing. It was September 2001. The doctor at the second clinic that day wasted no time in ordering x-rays, scans and whatever else was needed to see what was bringing on such pain. He had a good idea, though, as to what the problem was. He thought that she had a collapsed lung.

Looking back at that time, things seemed to move very quickly. Results came in and she found out that she had lung cancer. She was currently a non-smoker, but she smoked when she was in her early twenties, then quit for good a few years later. She was referred to a cancer specialist here in town, and the plan was that she would start radiation right away and then chemotherapy later if need be. There were a few more trips to the specialist's office as more results came in, but she never went on her own. Sometimes I would go with her, or sometimes our youngest sister Madelyn would. She was referred to the Oncology team at the Oshawa General Hospital, now currently Lakeridge Health.

To say Deborah's diagnosis sent shock waves through our family is a huge understatement. Not only did it devastate us, but it damn near killed us. We were reeling, all of us, not just those who were closest to her -- her mother and sisters -- but everyone. Her aunts, uncles, cousins, friends. Those who were close by, and those who were far away. Everyone was in shock. The news was like a meteor strike; we were at the core and took the brunt of it, but everyone else for miles around would feel it too.

Deb was scared, of course, we all were, but we tried very hard not to let her see it. And there were three little children who loved to spend time with their Auntie Deb, so we had to protect them somewhat from what the big people were worried about. Deborah moved back in with our Mum, which was a good move, as then there would always be someone about. We were all going to pull together and be strong for her and do whatever we could. I told her not to look at the whole picture because sometimes it was too scary; it was better to break it down and look at the smaller picture. One day at a time we would take it, all of us, together. In between radiation treatments, we tried to stick to a routine as much as possible. I would go to work in the mornings, then round to Mum's in the evenings to see how things were. Deb would go to her treatments, sometimes all of us would go with her, or only one of us would. Didn't matter who, as long as she wasn't alone. Other family members and friends would drop by to spend time with her as well, and her very favourite Aunt Jean, who was also her godmother, would make a surprise visit from Prince Edward Island that would lift all of our spirits.

Soon it was Christmastime and we had the best one we could possibly have under the circumstances. Deb was still going for radiation, but she really didn't look that unwell, she was really just tired. She had a lot of pain in her left arm, though, and at times she would have a hard time straightening it out. But she was doing okay and she was holding her own. The family tradition of all gathering round at Mum's house on Christmas Eve after Mass at St. Greg's continued, and there was much food, merriment and carol singing. It was a full house with all of us there, with husbands or boyfriends and with the three children about, it made for a lot of fun. We didn't know what the New Year would bring, but for now we counted our blessings that we were all together and happy.

After the New Year, Deb got the call from the doctor saying that she was to come in and see him, to discuss what the next steps in her treatment would be. So back we went, and the surgeon told us he was going to try to cut out part of the cancerous lung. Yes, he reassured us, she would be able to survive with part of her lung missing. We knew that people already could, though. Our Aunt Jean had a section of her lung removed decades before and she was still going strong and still a smoker. This was all positive news, and we were very hopeful and thankful that the doctor was giving us better news than we were used to getting.

Her surgery appointment was not long afterwards. We went up early in the morning to the hospital together and I waited with her in the room while she had her IV line put in and all the other pre-op things that they had to do. Then we sat and waited for them to come back and get her, and we kept ourselves distracted by making small talk. We talked about everything except for the surgery. Of course, though, no amount of small talk was going to take the worry away. I told her that she would be fine and had nothing to worry about. She was scared and so was I, but I tried not to let it show. Soon they came and wheeled her away to the operating room, and I went back to the waiting room to wait. And pray.

Hours had passed and there was no sign of anyone, and no news. I had read every sign on the walls, and all the magazines in the waiting room but absorbed nothing; I was just trying to keep myself distracted so my mind wouldn't wander too much. I called my Mum and told her that I was still waiting, and she said she was just on her way up and would be there shortly. It wasn't too long afterwards that the doctor came and took us from the waiting room to a nearby office. The look on his face told us that he didn't have good news to share, and that old familiar feeling of dread was starting to seep through me. He was sorry, he began, they had opened up her back but there was nothing they could do. The cancer had spread, he told us, and there was nothing he could cut out that would make any difference. She was now in the recovery room, recovering from a surgery that did absolutely nothing except to give her a false sense of hope. It would be a few hours before we could see her. A few hours to try to pull ourselves together.

Mum and I went outside, we had to just get out of the hospital, distance ourselves from what we had just been told. My legs could not support me, and I was having trouble standing. If I hadn't leaned myself up against a nearby pole, I would have fallen over. My mother was literally doubled over with shock. This was catastrophic. How could this be happening? How were we supposed to tell Deborah, let alone anyone else? We repeated the words to each other; maybe if we said them a few times, they would lose their shock value. They didn't. They sounded just as cruel, just as unfair as when we heard them the first time. The cancer was in her left lung, they opened her up to try to cut it out, but instead they found that it had spread everywhere. That would explain why she was having limited use of her left arm. Good God, how much worse could this get? Mum and I were with her in the hospital room when the doctor came in to tell her that the surgery to remove the tumour and part of her lung was unsuccessful. The cancer had spread, she was told, and they were going to start chemotherapy right away.

Instead of starting the chemo and watching her hair fall out, she and Madelyn decided to cut it off instead. They thought that it wouldn't be as bad if they did it first, if they got to her hair before the chemo did, but the crying that came upstairs from the basement told us they were wrong. Deb tried to stick to her regular routine, shopping, meeting up with people and playing with her nieces, and on the days in between her treatments, she wasn't too bad.

But as time went on, she became sicker and weaker. The treatments didn't really do a lot for her except tire her out and wear her down. She was admitted to the hospital for a period of time because she was having breathing issues, but we were looking forward to having her home for a few days in March. The hospital sent a huge bag of medication with her that she would need for the days at home, and as well, they sent someone from the home oxygen company to come meet me at Mum's to set up it up and show me how to work it. She tried, she really did, but she couldn't manage for more than one night. Even with the oxygen, she wasn't able to cope as well as everyone hoped, so there was no other choice but for her to go back to the hospital.

Her doctors wanted her to try more treatment, but she didn't want to and I don't blame her. She was a shell of the person she used to be, and it was hard to say what was draining her the fastest -- the cancer or the treatment for it. Madelyn lived out of town at the time but came back home and stayed at our Mum's to help out. I took a leave of absence from work and between Mum, Mad and I, and Caroline too, we stayed with Deb around the clock at the hospital. Our visits would overlap by ten minutes or so, so that there was not one moment that Deborah was alone.

Deb and I always used to have great fun,

laughing and carrying on, and we still did that as much as we could even at the hospital. I did not mind at all being there with her for hours on end; in fact, there was no person I would rather be with than with her. When she was up to it, she would still laugh and goof around, and it would do us all well to see her happy and smiling. Mum would tell me Deb would be in good spirits, and then the doctor would come in and tell her all this depressing news about tumours and to talk about palliative care plans and she would be destroyed all over again. And it would take a while for her to bounce back from all the bad news they kept continually telling her. Mum asked me if I could sort something out, so I asked the nurse if the team of doctors would meet with me, just so we could all be on the same page as each other. I told them we all knew that she didn't have a lot of time left, and Deborah knew it as well. Pick one day, and one doctor to go in there and say what needs to be said. And that would be it, no more. Tell me everything instead, and my mother agreed with that, too. Just stop coming by every two hours and repeating the same dire news to her. So that's what they did, and the steady stream of bad news not coming through the door every five minutes made a huge difference to everyone, but especially to Deb.

About a week later, one of the doctors stopped me on my way down the hall. As he directed me into his office, he said there was something else to discuss. As he pinned up the latest

X-ray of her lungs, he explained to me that the cancer was aggressive and spreading even quicker than they had originally thought. Tell me, I said, how much time does she have? He pointed out things on the X-rays that may have told him something but didn't tell me what I needed to know. Tell me, I asked him, the best you can, how much time does she have left? Just tell me.

Maybe, he said, maybe four to six weeks.

When is the right time to tell someone something like this? Which was greater, my right to keep it from her, or her right to know the severity of her illness? It wasn't really my right to keep anything from her, I knew that. It was her right to know, but at the same time, I wanted to protect her. It was an impossible question to answer, and impossible to ask anyone else. There was really only my mother that I felt any obligation to, other than Deb, to talk about this to. And I knew what my mother would say. Don't tell Deborah, don't take away what little hope she might have left.

In a roundabout way, Deb herself guided me in this difficult decision. Before she was moved to a private room, she shared a room with an older lady whose bed was directly across from hers. Her husband and son were in to see her just as much as our family was in to see Deb. We saw them all the time and would nod hello to each other in passing. One day, I was just getting into Deb's room and the other patient was sound asleep. The husband and son were talking in hushed tones. Deb motioned for me to be quiet and then told me when they were gone that the husband and son had received some bad news and they didn't know what to do. Their loved one's cancer had spread, and they didn't know if they should tell her or not, and they were torn about what to do. I could totally relate to that but, of course, didn't tell my sister that I was in the same predicament.

When I came in the next day, the family was visiting again. Everyone seemed cheerful and chipper, husband, son and mother laughing and smiling as usual. When they left, I asked Deb what happened. She said they decided not to tell her, and the end result was that they carried on as they did before and there was no additional upset caused. I cautiously said to my sister, you know what, I think they did the right thing. Deb told me that she thought so, too. So I got an answer to my dilemma. I didn't tell her what the doctors had told me, and a huge burden was lifted from my shoulders. Deb knew that her time here with us was limited anyway, as we all did. What she didn't have was the time frame that the doctors had given me. Deborah accepted her fate better than we could ever hope to. She had great faith and she accepted that God knew what was best for her, and she never questioned it and she never complained about what life had handed her. She and I would have long talks and she would tell me things that I didn't want to hear but that she needed to say. Make sure I'm buried with Dad she would tell me, and take care of Mum too.

And Lise, don't forget about the letter. All of this I am agreeing to and reassuring her that I will do as she asks. In my mind though, I am thinking that I can't cope, and that I don't want her saying things like this to me. Most of all, I don't want her to see me cry.

I will do all of this Deb, I tell her, you have my word.

Chapter 9 ~ All at Sea

By the spring of that year I was mostly at the hospital around the clock. I would come up at lunch time, stay 'til the evening, go home and change, and head back up there and stay overnight with Deborah. We all pitched in, but it was getting harder and harder to make ourselves go up and see her. She was declining, and it was so hard to see a vibrant young woman who was the thread in the fabric of our family, who filled us with her laughter and her music, wind down. Day by day it got harder to watch her slip away from us, and we were powerless to do anything about it. Caroline hadn't been able to cope with visiting for a while now, and that was okay; it was too hard on her to be there. Didn't mean she loved Deb any less, but her coping abilities, which were never strong to begin with, were waning. My mother was having a very hard time with all of this. Of course she would, and as hard as it was for us, it must have been simply devastating for her. She came up and stayed, though, and put a brave face on and tried to do what she could. But she was in denial, I could see that. I don't think she could fully accept that we were losing Deb. And I could understand that too. How terrible this time must have been for her. She tried her best though, and when April 2nd came along, it was Deborah's birthday. Even as adults, we all got together and Mum always had cakes for us on our birthdays. So when Deb's birthday came, Mum brought her good dishes up to the hospital and we wheeled Deb to one of the side rooms and we all had some cake together. Instead of the normal feeling of celebration, it was just heartbreaking and horrendous. The absolute futility of it and my Mum trying her best to bring some sort of normal to the whole situation by bringing the fancy dishes and a small birthday cake to the hospital was heartbreaking for all of us. A mother trying to do the best for her firstborn child, on what we all knew would be her last birthday. I don't break easily and never cried once at that hospital, and I was able to put on a brave face for everyone -- Deborah, my younger sisters and my mother. But that day I excused myself from the room with some lame excuse, went down the hall and locked myself in the washroom and cried my eyes out.

A couple of evenings later, I was to meet Madelyn in the parking lot of the church which was a block from the hospital. It was our meet-up place and dropping-off point, and I was going home and she was going up. But she was crying, she couldn't make herself go up there for her time with Deb, it was getting too hard. But she didn't want Deb to be alone. Our Mum was there now, and I needed to go home to change. I told her that it was okay, Deb would understand and I would go back up so Mum could go home and get some rest.

Deb slipped in and out of consciousness that

evening. She had been moved to a private room and it was very quiet, just the steady hum of the monitors, even the television that was usually on in her room was switched off. No other patients and their families to talk to, no other families and their dilemmas to distract us. So I just sat there and thought back at all that we shared and about all that we had been through together. How was I going to ever live without her? How would any of us? Should I call our mother? Would Deb want Mum there to see her at this time? Would it be too hard for Mum to even be there with Deb like this? I didn't know what to do; I never seemed to know what to do anymore, every decision overwhelmed me, so I climbed into her bed and lay down beside her. It was nighttime now, and I didn't think she would see the morning. She was slowing down and her life was leaving her. Her last words were that she was going to sleep now, that she was tired.

Sleep, sweet sister, sleep.

Early that morning, just as the sun was rising and four days after her 40th birthday, our Deborah slipped peacefully from this life into the next. I went out to the nurses' station and told them that she was gone, and one of them came into the room to check on her. I made a few phone calls, and my mother and our family Priest arrived at the hospital at the same time, with Caroline and Madelyn arriving not too long afterwards. We stayed with Deb for a little while, all of us really just too sad to say anything. There were no words that would fill the void, nothing to fill the hollowness. After my Mum and sisters left, I stayed with Deb for a bit longer.

I didn't want to leave her.

I didn't want her to leave me.

*****

My Dad's death taught me about horror, hatred and fear. My sister's death eleven years later taught me how short life could be, and her dying terrified me. I was already well schooled in the reality of how fleeting life really was and on how short our time here could be. But what I learned after my sister's death was that it's not what you have in this life that matters, it's who you have.

A year after my sister died, I packed up and moved away. I knew I would be back, though. I had made promises that I had every intention of keeping.

Pictures

My great-grandfather William Johnson who perished in the Halifax Explosion along with his wife, son and baby daughter.

My Nana Madeline Johnson (foreground), with her brothers and sisters, Halifax, Nova Scotia. She would lose most of her family in the Halifax Explosion of 1917.

Roland Slingerland, 10 years old

*My father joined the Royal Canadian Navy when he was
17 years old*

*The Canadian icebreaker HMCS Labrador, the first large
vessel to transit the Northwest Passage*

A replica of the Blue Nose that my father built

My Mum and Dad, early days, Pictou, Nova Scotia

Abner, Alden, Roland (Slinger) Slingerland, Preston 1957

My Dad with the Stewart boys, Pictou, Nova Scotia, 1957

*The ribbon from my Dad's Navy cap, which I would later
take with me to Frontenac Prison. Dad is the man
pictured in the right of the photo, as he was featured in
a book about the Northwest Passage*

Grandma Slingerland with Dad and me. The lobster claw ashtray that he made is shown on the table

Although we met under tragic circumstances many years before, Greg O'Driscoll has become a valued and trusted friend

Some of the good people who surround me: Top L- with my friend Kim, R- my great pal Freda; bottom L, a day out with Sussex friends

My father during his Navy Days

Me and my big sister Deb, 1970, Oshawa, Ontario

Top L- My Uncle Bert Duford, one of my father's long time friends Top R- My Aunt Jean DesRoches

Bottom- My Mum and my Aunt Margy Somers

My Dad pictured shortly before his murder

OSHAWA

Have you seen murder suspect?

Durham Regional Police are seeking the public's assistance in tracing the whereabouts over the past month of John Terrance Porter, 31, who has been charged with first-degree murder in the death of Roland Slingerland, 58, of Oshawa. Police said Porter also wears glasses on occasion. Anyone with information is asked to call police at 579-1520 (ext. 211).

Durham Regional Police issued this notice to the public looking for information on John Terrence Porter, charged with First Degree Murder

In Memory of Dad

Roland "Slinger" Slingerland
August 23, 1932-February 5, 1991
RCN-HMCS Labrador-Wallaceburg-
La Hulloise-Ontario

It has been 24 years since
our Dad was brutally murdered.

We are asking the Parole Board of
Canada and Correctional Services
Canada to make reasonable changes
to their Policies and Procedures to
better protect the personal details of
Victims of Crime.

**Offenders should not be entitled to
something as precious as a
Victim's Identity.**

To see our Open letter to the
Parole Board go to
www.facebook.com/justice4dad

*In this memoriam I publicly asked for the public's
support, and wrote my letter to the Parole Board of
Canada accessible through a QR code*

Chapter 10 ~ As the Crow Flies

The wind slammed the door behind me as I carried the last two pumpkins to the front porch. A few nights before, we had the massive pumpkin carving festival at our house, and even though we had spread newspapers on the table, I was still finding little slippery white seeds everywhere. I looked at the end result of the pumpkin I carved, and I was pretty sure it wouldn't scare anyone – it looked more comical than spooky, but it would do. I just had to find a few more tea light candles for later, so the trick or treaters would be better able to see our carving skills.

Now that it was Halloween, there was a definite change to the weather. There was a crispness to the air, not quite the harsh bite of winter yet, though that would come; but for now there was just a nip to let us know that the seasons were changing. And that was okay by me. I love the fall and, after the heat of the summertime, Autumn was a welcome visitor, bringing with her a coolness that would extinguish the remaining embers of a hot and sultry summer. The trees would be alive with colour, if only for a short time, but during that time, what a performance they would give! Dark green leaves magically turning to hues of red, gold, yellow and orange. And with the wind blowing and branches swaying, the leaves would then do their graceful dance into a downward spiral, falling to the ground as the trees shrugged off their colourful coats.

I went back to my mental checklist: Pumpkins done, check. Decorations out, check. Fill witch's cauldron with treats, check. Claire was having her friend and her brother over; along with their mother they were meeting up at our house later so they could all go out trick or treating together, so I wanted to get as much done as I could before they came over. The biggest task facing me that evening, though, was one I'm sure that parents everywhere were facing. How to convince a five-year-old that she had to wear warm clothes underneath her witch's costume. The trick every Halloween was to find an equal balance of warm layers but at the same time having the child still be able to move their arms. It was our yearly Halloween obstacle.

Somewhere in between stringing white cottony spider webs in the hedge and hanging little dangling skeletons from the dining room chandelier, I finally took a moment to sit down. I grabbed a quick drink and collected the mail that I had dumped on the hallway table earlier in the day.

Sifting through the usual bills, pizza deals and flyers, I came across an official looking letter addressed to myself from a return address that I didn't recognize. Some government branch of something or other, I figured. I opened it and as I read the first few lines, I could feel my heart grow heavy in my chest simultaneously with a sinking feeling that formed in my stomach: it was a letter from the Parole Board of Canada. The man who murdered my father twenty years before was applying for escorted temporary absences from the prison in Kingston, Ontario, where he was incarcerated. I was informed that there was to be a Panel Hearing in January 2012. I could submit a Victim Impact Statement to them with the option to present it in person or by video.

I couldn't believe what I was reading. Here it was, Halloween night, and my own personal demons were coming back to haunt me. My past was colliding with my present life, and despite my best efforts, I was woefully unprepared for it.

Shortly afterwards, my husband came in the front door, home from work for the day. He could see something was wrong, and I showed him the letter. And as he was trying to read it, I was rambling in the background, telling him that I wasn't able to take part in Halloween that night. Claire could go out, I decided, with her friend and her brother, along with their mother, and that would free him up to stay home and hand out the treats. Light was fading and it would soon be dark enough for the children to start coming round.

As for me, I was going to lay face down in my bed.

I felt sick and my head was starting to hurt.

Plan B, I decided, was to just leave bowls of candy on the porch and shut off the lights and go lay down -- then Halloween would be done. Nick wasn't having any of that, though. Let's just get through Halloween, he said, and then we could go over the letter again later. He was going to take Claire out with her friends as planned and I would give out candy at the door as I did every year. Along with numerous witches, ghosts and goblins, Halloween came and went, and I did my duty at the door, but anytime there was a lull between trick or treaters, my mind went right back to that letter. I could already see the black clouds forming on the horizon.

I had met and married my second husband, a quiet, reserved Englishman six years before. To say he was typically English was an understatement. He was a tea drinking, level-headed, quick thinking man with a cracking sense of humour. Together we had a little girl Claire, and my girl Kayla from my first marriage, who was Claire's big sister by nine years. Despite the age gap, they got on well and found a lot of common interests despite the years between them. So together the four of us, complete with a German Shepherd and a bunny rabbit named Daisy, lived together in a house that was a few blocks away from the one I grew up in. At first I thought that maybe moving back to the same area wouldn't be such a great idea; I had lots of good memories, but there were a lot of bad ones mixed in with them, too. But I found comfort in taking my children to the same neighbourhood park that my sisters and I played in when we were younger. And somewhere, I was sure, my father was smiling as Nick and Claire would take one of their ambling walks down to the creek, Claire with her Tinkerbell fishing rod slung over her shoulder.

So I had come full circle. I had gotten far away and stayed away, but when it was time to come back home, I moved right back to where my life began. There were a few of the original families still left on my old street, and I couldn't believe that the little kids that I baby-sat when I was a teenager were now grown and had children of their own. How could that be? It meant one thing, of course: I was getting older and the changes of time had occurred in my absence.

But it was as if that letter from the Parole Board took a life of its own. What were they talking about? Only 20 years have gone by, what was wrong with these people? Can't they do the math? The original sentence was life imprisonment with no eligibility of parole for 25 years. By my calculation, they were about five years too early to be contacting me about anything, bar a prison break or riot or something along that line. No mention of entitlement to escorted temporary absences on the original certificate of conviction. I wasn't even sure what they were.

And there I was, a mere six months earlier thinking that I would get the jump on the Parole Board. I really didn't know where to start, but I knew eventually that I would have to reach out and begin the daunting task of preparing my family and myself for the prospect of parole. If I was trying to drag the years out, I'm sure the man who killed my father was willing them to pass. Maybe he was sitting in a prison somewhere, crossing off the lines of his jail sentence on his cell wall. Sure, I told myself, that and hammering out license plates and only getting meals of bread and water too. So I figured I would give myself a lot of time to prepare for when the parole process would begin for him, 25 years into his life sentence. Parole. Even saying the word could get my blood boiling. It wasn't like our family ever would get parole, of course not, our sentence and our Dad's sentence was the only true life one handed out in the courtroom that long ago day years before. His parole eligibility date of 2016 might as well have been tattooed somewhere on my body, as it was ingrained in every fibre of my being.

Before I got that letter that Halloween night, I had finally found the right people to talk to that would put me in touch with the parole board. Through the years, there was no contact from the parole board at all. How could there be, really, they wouldn't know where to reach me, and I wouldn't know where to reach them. There was nothing set up at the time of Dad's murder, no registry with contact numbers, nothing that we were aware of. So six months before I got the letter from the Parole Board on Halloween night, I had gone back to the person who had helped so much at the beginning of it all, and that was Greg O'Driscoll. He was still in the area and part of the Crown's office, but he was now the Crown Attorney for Durham Region. I had last spoken to him maybe a decade before when I was getting ready to move, leaving him my contact details for just in case. He was my only link to the past and I really didn't know who else to call. It was good to talk to Greg again; we had a good catch-up on the phone about things. He gave me the number of Victim Services of Durham Region, which was linked through the Durham Regional Police. I promised to keep him updated over the next while as the parole date of 2016 got closer: it wasn't just me who had a vested interest in what Terry Porter was doing.

The person I spoke to at Victim Services was very helpful as I explained to her what I was doing, and she listened intently to my story. There had been no contact between our family and the Parole Board ever, and this case ended years ago, and the man had been in prison (we hoped) for almost twenty years. I continued on, saying that I was giving myself a lot of time to mentally prepare myself, my Mum and sisters for the eventuality of parole. It was a long way off still, five years away, but I wanted to get all my ducks in a row.

The help I received that day and continued to receive from the Victim Support Services was monumental. Anything I asked, anything I ran by them, if they didn't know the answer to it, they would find me someone who did. I had a lot of questions, twenty years' worth, but they answered them with patience and a genuine interest in my situation. They were my go-to people, and I tapped their resources many times over. Jade and the rest of the team made the task of tracking down resources easier and gave me good ideas when I would ask for suggestions of who else I could contact in regards to other hurdles that I came across.

Victim Services had given me the number to the Parole Board of Canada, and it was through their office, I was told, that I would receive whatever information I was entitled to. If I needed anything else, I was to feel free to call back the support services and they would help me as best as they could.

I called the number of the Parole Board and explained my situation to the person who answered the phone and fielded my inquiry. I gave the full name of the Offender, John Terrance Porter, but I was told that I would have to register with them as a victim before I could receive any information about him. Stop right there, I said, I'm not registering as a victim. Why would I do that? I'll register with the Parole Board, but not as a victim. I never was one and I never would be, I told her, my Dad was the victim. I was adamant -- I was not going to register as one and I didn't think that I should have to. After all, I spent the last twenty years not thinking of myself as one, why should I have to put my name on a registered victim's list now? Detective MacDonald's words all those years before had made

131

an impact on me, and in my mind, they were a big reason why I got through the ensuing years somewhat intact.

No, I told the Parole Board, you weren't registering me as a victim, no way, no how.

I registered as a victim with the Parole Board of Canada two weeks later. I had to, and although it went against every grain in my body to say I was a victim of anything, I knew I had to register with them to get whatever information I was entitled to. And this information wasn't just for me; it was for my family, too. And besides, I told myself, victim was just a word. It was how it was interpreted and how you perceived yourself that gave it meaning. As my birthday was during the beginning of May, it made me a Taurus, and I had the stubborn persona typical for those born under this astrological sign. So even though I didn't like it, I gave in and provided the Parole Board my details. And, as I liked to remind people who mentioned my stubbornness in the past and my unmoving mindset about things, that being stubborn was a good thing, an enviable asset people should want to have. It was just, I learned, that while it was good to be stubborn, the trick of it was to know where and when to apply it. In other words, you can't fight every battle: save your fighting for the ones that mattered the most.

But by contacting the Parole Board and registering with them, it was if the floodgates opened. After all this time, there were people who could tell me some of the answers to what I had been wondering about for the past twenty years. Terry Porter was currently incarcerated at Frontenac Prison, just outside of Kingston, Ontario, which was about 266km (163 miles) east of Toronto. It was a medium security facility. The upcoming panel hearing was for Escorted Temporary Absence (ETAs) from the prison and could be for any number of reasons. They could be for medical or personal reasons; I wasn't allowed to know the specifics, though. And the hearing could be canceled or rescheduled at any time by the offender. I could also do a Victim Impact Statement which could be submitted in writing, or by audio or video. I could also present it orally at the hearing.

So not only were the floodgates opened by registering, it was as if a dam had burst and there was nothing but torrential rain in the forecast. I was receiving a lot of information from the Parole Board, I would read it all over, call the communications officer and talk to her or leave a message for her if she wasn't in. I would always get a prompt reply, and they would always deal with me courteously. They had sent me a statement checklist which was a guideline to writing a Victim Impact Statement. It was the size of a regular sheet of paper, divided down the middle with a Do and a Do Not side. The 'do' side was pretty basic, do write about physical harm, ongoing medical needs, ongoing emotional harm, and describe the effect of the crime on your daily life. They also advised

Victims of Crime to keep it brief -- a few pages or about ten minutes when read aloud. I had already decided that I would write a Victim Impact Statement and, without a doubt, I would present it myself in person. But how was I supposed to condense all their guidelines into a ten-minute period of time? Impossible! Twenty years of hell in ten minutes? No way, I had too much to say.

It was now the middle of November, Halloween was long gone, and soon Christmas would be upon us. So I tried to figure out how much time I had to get my mind around all that was happening, how much time there was before the yet undated panel hearing in January. At the most, I would have about six or seven weeks to write a Victim Impact Statement as they wanted it thirty days before the hearing: ten weeks to get my head around seeing my father's killer again, and ten short weeks to mentally prepare to re-open all this again. I had already made the decision not to tell my Mum and sisters about the hearing; my Christmas was ruined, why ruin everyone else's? No, I would keep quiet about the whole thing. I knew for certain that neither my mother or Caroline would come to the hearing anyway, nor Madelyn, as she was living out west. No, Nick and I would go up to Kingston ourselves, spend the night there, have one of our friends stay at the house overnight with the girls. The children were to know nothing about it either. How, I wondered, was I going to be able to cope with all this, let alone get it done within six to ten weeks at what was supposed to be the Most Wonderful Time of the Year?

I was assigned a Regional Communications Officer from the Parole Board who would help guide me through this process. And I would speak to her often, and I came to like her as well, but to my mind, she worked for the Parole Board, therefore 'them', and I was, well, just me, trying to do my best to wade through the onslaught of information they gave me.

The Parole Board didn't know what date in January 2012 that the hearing would be as they didn't have their calendars set that far in advance, but as soon as they knew, I would know. I asked them how come this is happening now, instead of at the twenty-five year mark of his sentence? After all, that is what we had been comforting ourselves with for the last two decades. This man was sentenced to life and with no parole eligibility for 25 years, the parole process surely would begin then, not four or five years sooner. They explained that there were no full parole opportunities for twenty-five years. There were, apparently, different kinds of things that he was eligible for before that point. Pity, no one seems to realize that, I told her, not just the victim's family, but it was a pretty widespread assumption with the public as well, parole means parole. Say what you mean, and mean what you say. If you mean that the twenty-five-year eligibility is for FULL parole, then by all means say it. Write it down on certificates of conviction before you hand them over to families who will look at that piece of paper in the years to come, gathering what comfort they can from it. If you mean that forms of parole start at the twenty-one-year mark of a life sentence, why aren't you saying that? All I was looking for was truth in sentencing, and already it failed me, but it shouldn't have, though. Truth in sentencing should have started with the federal document that was given to me all those years ago. But it didn't.

In my mind, I would come to refer to the Parole Board as the 'Mighty Parole Board.' As a regular, everyday news-watching, newspaper-reading Canadian, to me they seemed to be responsible for many wrong moves in the past. Now, with my past as the daughter of a murdered man coming to the forefront, I shifted from the regular everyday Canadian to someone who would deal with the Mighty Parole Board firsthand. I would see the intricate workings of their system, and try to muddle my way through it. Who were these panelists that would render such big decisions about who would stay in prison and who would start on the path to reintegration into society? Were any of them regular everyday people? Or, I wondered, were some of them people like me, who were touched by a horrific crime, who would take their experiences to the table? Were they lawyers, judges, doctors? Did these panelists represent an accurate cross section of the Canadian public, who, I believe, should be well represented as it was to them, the everyday people of Canada, that these offenders would one day be returned to? I found that the Parole Board wasn't answerable to anyone, certainly not to me, and not to the Canadian public either.

The Governor in Council, I would learn, appointed panelists upon the recommendation of Public Safety Canada. Panelists can be either part time or full time, and their terms are either three or five years in length. They require a minimum of five years experience in a decision-making environment, with knowledge of the criminal justice system. They also require a degree from a recognized university in one of the disciplines comprising the human sciences; for example, law, criminology, social work, psychology etc. As well, they will consider those with a combination of relevant education, job-related training and/or experience. The Board, I was told, makes every effort to recruit people from a wide variety of cultural, ethnic and professional backgrounds to ensure a balanced representation of the community.

But I think that communities aren't just defined by people who are highly educated and well paid, but communities embrace all walks of life and are made up of people with varying life experiences to contribute. I wondered if there were people on the Board who would be classified by the Board's own definition as a victim of crime. People like me, everyday people, and I am sure there are lots of them, who have, by no choice of their own, been touched by a violent crime. Their life experiences and their insights would be a valuable tool to the decision-making process of the Parole Board. I wonder what the results would be if the Parole Board asked ten random people off the street and had them sit in at a panel hearing. I wonder what the results and recommendations of this randomly chosen cross-section of the community would be, and if their decisions would mirror the same as the Parole Board's decision on things?

The victim statement check list the Parole Board sent me also had a Do Not side as well to it. Do not address the offender directly when writing or reading your statement. Do not use profanities or disrespectful language. Do not threaten anyone, including the Offender. Do not include music, images, graphics, other people or other elements in any video or audio recording of the statement. To me, the Offender was coming off pretty well in the Do Not list. Don't swear, don't address him directly, and don't bring any pictures or graphics with you: no pictures of loved ones, no graphic crime scene photos. No, nothing, I thought, that might remind the Offender of his crime or of the person he killed. No, I thought, we wouldn't want to traumatize him now, would we?

By this time I had the communications officer at the Parole Board's direct number on speed-dial. Let me just clarify a few things, I said. How come I can't bring a picture of my Dad? This is the offender's hearing, I was told, not my father's. The offender has been convicted and sentenced for

138

his crime, and the point of the hearing is assessing how far he has come in regards to rehabilitation. I was also told that when writing my impact statement that I didn't need to go into the details of the crime. Why not? I asked. I thought the crime was the reason this man was sent to prison, and hence the panel hearing all these years later? I was told that it was just a suggestion not to include those details, but the panelists have heard things like it before. I was to focus on the impact the crime had on my life. Well, then, I thought to myself, I would need more than ten minutes to speak; my impact statement would need to be more than a few pages long and I would need a hell of a lot more than six weeks to write it and to prepare myself to present it. I could feel all the long ago anger that I hoped I had contained years before rise up again, stoked by every conversation I would have with the Parole Board.

But true to their word, the Parole Board called to let me know the date the Panel Hearing was set for.

It was scheduled for Friday, January 13th, 2012.

Of course, the first person I went to pick up the phone to call and tell about all this was my sister Deb. She had been gone for almost ten years now, and somehow I managed, as we all did, to keep her in my heart and memories, but to go on with my life. But I needed her now, I needed her guidance and input, and I needed her beside me at that Panel

Hearing. She and I would have gone to Kingston together, there was absolutely no doubt about that. So I didn't just have to get things right for myself, but I had to get things right for her as well. Because even though I couldn't see her, I could feel her around me, and that was a whole different kind of pain because I feel her but couldn't reach her. If wishing alone could bring a person back to life again, she would have been standing beside me, and would be standing beside me still. And I would wake up through the night with tears on my face from crying for her. I would surprise people when I would tell them that losing my sister was a thousand times harder than losing my Dad. Easily. We were very close and she and I were each other's support through our Dad's murder, and now she was gone. And I needed her so much. She alone was the only person who knew the full horror of the whole story, and we both leaned on the other all those years ago. I needed someone who could relate to what I was going through, someone to talk to about things, and to help me. And, in the absence of my sister, that task would fall to Greg O'Driscoll.

We met again for the first time in 20 years on a cold November morning at his office. Seeing Greg again was like opening a door and walking backwards into the past. He had changed, and so had I, but he was still the same nice man that I met all those years before and still very easy to talk to. After completing the bar exam in early 1985 he commenced his career with the Ministry of the

Attorney General/Crown Attorney's office and prosecuted as an assistant crown for the first 25 years, and for the past 6 years has been the Crown Attorney for Durham Region. He told me that he had never forgot Terry Porter or my father's brutal murder, reflecting that my father was a very hardworking gentleman whose life was viciously cut short by a psychopath. He also said that he always thought that my father was honourable as well, putting his life on the line to save someone else's. It will never be known if my father knew the location of Terry Porter's girlfriend or if he did and by not revealing it, he likely saved her life. By meeting and spending some time with Greg, he was able to provide me with something that no one else could give me: a connection. With the absence of my sister, Greg was my direct link to the past, someone that fully knew what kind of person I was dealing with. He knew inside out the horrors of the crime; I didn't have to worry about him feeling sorry for me, I didn't have to think about shocking him with details of my father's death because he knew it all already. It was a comfort to go in and talk to him, knowing that I could speak freely and not worry about upsetting him with what I said. I had come to a point many years ago where I could talk about my father's murder quite factually, with very little emotion. It, of course, didn't mean that I didn't feel things, of course I did, how could I not. I just rarely wore my emotions on my sleeve anymore, not in front of anyone anyway, but when left alone with my thoughts, I could get very emotional. And that worked both ways with Greg and me: he could speak freely to me about the horrors of this crime without thinking that it would be too much for me to handle. We talked about the brutality of Terry Porter's crime, and his lifelong anger issues. My father's death wasn't quick, we agreed, as Terry Porter killed my dad over an extended, prolonged brutal attack. Speaking to Greg that morning and in future meetings always left me feeling the same: not quite as alone in all of this, and that I had one of the good guys on my side. Actually, I had one of the very best men on my side, and I am forever grateful for the role he has played in my life. And, although we didn't meet under ideal circumstances, in the years since, he has become more than the prosecutor from all those years before; instead he has become a valued, trusted friend.

Through all of this, I was working full time in the Nursing Department of a very busy and at times very stressful Long-Term Care facility and I could feel the pressure of everything getting on top of me. I was trying to raise my two girls and trying to keep appearing as my normal happy self through it all. I was having trouble, though; I could see it and I could feel it. Christmas was on the doorstep and it was usually my favourite time of year, but this year I could care less if it came or not. And I could feel the old anger coming back again, and I didn't want that; there was no room in my life for that kind of rage anymore. I had built a decent, normal life for myself and I was proud that I came out of the nightmare of my Dad's murder a happy, well-adjusted person. Deb and Dad were gone, but instead of focusing on whom I had lost, I tried to think about who I still had. I tried not to look at my father and sister as losses, but instead to focus on what I had gained from having them in my life to start with. Not that it was an easy process, or an easy thing to do, and I could feel all that slipping away now. They were gone, but with everything being stirred up, and so suddenly, both of them were on my mind again almost constantly. Their voices were not just confined in my head but seemed to ricochet in every room I went into, every familiar street I walked down. I was heavy with the thought of them; they both were always there beneath the surface and quiet for so long, but now they both wanted to be heard again. I had huge doubts that I could be their voices, and daily I was finding it hard just to silence my own voice in my head, never mind all the other people that were vying for my attention. I had carried my father and my sister for years in my heart, but now they were in my heart and on my mind in equal measure.

And there was still the Victim Impact Statement to write. I would sit down, start it, rip it up and then start all over again. I tried many times, but I was finding it extremely difficult to find the words to convey my feelings, likely because I was feeling so many feelings at the same time --

sadness, anger, despair and reliving the loss all over again. They wanted me to write how Terry Porter's crime impacted me, but they were using the word impacted in the past sense; it was still impacting me and always would. To get things on paper was next to impossible and I put a lot of pressure on myself. Because if I didn't get it right, I would feel like I was letting everyone down.

I needed time off from work. That was a whole different kind of stress, and I couldn't write this statement and then go to work as well. What I don't think people understand is that you have to be in a certain place to write something like this. I had to get back into the head of my 22-year-old self and revisit her again, revisit her anguish and feel her pain again. That was the only way I could do it, though, and I knew it would hurt to look back, to be that girl again. So I took some time off work and gave myself a deadline: I wanted to have the Victim Impact Statement finished and mailed off to Kingston one week before Christmas. Then I could salvage what was left of the holidays and try to spend some time with those who were still here, and put the ones who weren't in the back of my mind, if only for a little while.

I also knew that I would need some professional help, too. I was feeling myself fall apart, and I struggled daily with the thought that I would lose myself, my current self, through all of this. I had great friends, people who loved and supported me, but I knew that alone wasn't going to

144

be enough. I needed someone who had experience with trauma, and who could help me deal with revisiting anguish after so much time. I picked up the phone and dialed Durham Victim Services to see if they had any ideas.

Of course they did. Victim Services were my go-to people for so very much, and after years of feeling that I spoke some sort of foreign language in regards to my father's murder and very few able to understand me, the people at Victim Services changed that. All of a sudden, I found people who not only spoke the same dialect as I did, but they were fluent in it. So I talked to Jade, told her that I needed some help. I didn't go into details with what I was struggling with at the time; I only told her that I was feeling that things were starting to get on top of me. She phoned me back with the number of a former nurse who was also a counselor and helped people deal with this kind of thing. I didn't know what exactly I was going through, but I really didn't think I was the best person to assess myself anymore. And that was a change, because through the years I had mostly just relied on myself and my own judgment for things. That's how badly shaken I was about the upcoming Panel Hearing; it threw me right off the steady path that I had trod along so well for such a long time.

Making the phone call to make the appointment was the easy part; actually keeping the appointment was the hard part. And I almost called to cancel it a couple of times leading up to it. I didn't want anyone to know about things, I've always dealt with problems on my own, and I had come out of this nightmare pretty well, I thought. But I kept the appointment and surprised myself by going back about once every two to three weeks from January to May. She knew what she was talking about, and she did help me. One day as I followed her down to her office, she said, 'You do know, Lisa, that your anger precedes you by at least five minutes.' Yes, I knew that. That was one of my bigger fears, that I would never be able to put all the stirred-up anger back to wherever I had stashed it away for all those years. It was like finding a key and unlocking a door that was bolted shut for a long, long time. The part of my mind that didn't want to revisit all these feelings, all this trauma, was on the other side of the door pushing to keep someone from getting in. And behind that door to the room, there was a fire building and some of the smoke was starting to seep through the bottom of the door. And here she was, this trauma nurse trying all these different keys to see which one would fit. I just hoped that once the door slowly swung open, that I would be able to close it again. So we would talk, and she would talk me through the panel hearing process as best as she could, and she would share her insights about things. Did I get anything out of it? Yes, I did, or I wouldn't have gone back. One of the biggest things I got from it was that I wasn't feeling quite as isolated anymore: there were people out there who knew exactly what I was feeling and what it might be like to be me.

Through the day, and half the night, too, different questions would come to mind. I would call the communications officer and run things past her. If she wasn't available, there was always someone else there to answer my questions. And with every phone call and every interaction, one thing became very clear to me: I had little or no control about anything. It was very much Terry Porter's hearing as they already told me. Even the smallest details were controlled: if they weren't saying that it was Terry Porter's hearing, they were telling me that some of the changes I wanted would be up to the panelists on the day of the hearing.

It was important for me to know how things would proceed at the panel hearing so I could best prepare myself for it, as I didn't want to be caught off guard by anything that I could easily sort out beforehand. So I asked at what point of the hearing I would be presenting my statement. At the beginning, came the response. I didn't want to speak first, I told them, I wanted to speak last, so the panelists would still have my voice in their heads when they went off to make their decision about Terry Porter's escorted absences. The Parole Board eventually conceded and told me that I would be able to present my statement, not at the start of the hearing but second to last, speaking before Terry Porter would. I was satisfied with that and confirmed that I would stand and speak right before he would. Well, no, I was told, you don't stand up at all; you read your statement while you are seated.

Well, no, sorry, but I don't think so. I told them that I would like to stand and speak, no one reads a speech while sitting down. My mind went back to the last time I did any public speaking. Ah, yes, Grade 6, in elementary school, it was part of the dreaded public speaking part of the curriculum we had to do. My speech was one I had written about dogs and I was standing up, not sitting down when I read it out loud to my teacher and classmates. I felt that the Parole Board was giving me the opportunity to read a victim statement, but just. You, sit down over there, and you can say what you need to first, as we are saving the real focus of this hearing until the last. Did anyone say this to me directly? No, not at all. But not only did I read the Do and Do Not Victim Checklist they gave me, but I could also very clearly see what they weren't giving me: any tools that I could use that would make my voice louder, clearer and stronger on that day.

The regional communications officer called me a few days before the hearing to inform me that the Parole Board of Canada conceded, and that I would be able to stand while reading my Victim Impact Statement.

And whoever thought that a Grade 6 speech on dogs would serve me so well in the future?

Finally I finished writing out my Victim Impact Statement. It was very hard to do, and I was very emotional when writing it. I read it to myself many times, read it out loud to my husband to see if it flowed all right. In my mind, I had to get this right, not just for myself but for my family. There is no wrong way to write an impact statement, of course, as everyone's experiences are different. But I tried to nail down the horror of Terry Porter's crime, the impact of our father's death on his children and the reasons why I thought that Terry Porter should be denied any form of parole. I couldn't do any better than what I did, and mailed it away to the Parole Board. They, of course, needed a copy a month beforehand. And they had the right to veto it and send it back to me to redo if need be. It was no longer a statement, and I would come to refer to it as a script, because that's what it was becoming. And as well, victims were to read an exact copy of what they sent in to the Parole Board for the hearing. No adding things on, I guess, no going overboard with emotion and just saying what you feel in the heat of the moment, I was just to read what was scripted in front of me.

So it was no surprise to me really when they called and said there was a part of the statement that I couldn't read. I thought that it might have been too graphic, but that wasn't the change they wanted me to make. Astonishingly, the part that they objected to was the heading that I put at the beginning of my statement that reads as follows:

"*I would like to make the Parole Board aware that we did not know that statements and personal letters of protest could be submitted to the*

149

Offender's file. So please don't think we've been silent all these years, please don't think we've forgotten our Dad and how much he meant to us."

So where exactly was the problem? I had written nothing offensive, included nothing graphic. I was told that they didn't like my use of the words "we" and "we've" in the statement I submitted. Why not? I asked. Because, I was told, it implied more than one person. Sigh. Well, yes, that is correct, I said, and that is what I meant. We, as in collectively, we as in family, friends, relatives and myself. And it was true, none of us knew that statements and personal letters of protest could be submitted to an Offender's file. The communications officer then told me that their concern was that by that by using the words "we" and "we've", they could act as a trigger for the offender.

WHAT?

If words might be a trigger for him, I said, they should halt any plans right now for the panel hearing. Cancel it, because this man is no use to anyone outside of a prison setting. Out in the real world, people use words all the time. Words are part of life on the outside, and it can be a big bad place of not only adjectives but verbs, nouns, pronouns as well. My flippancy aside, I was fuming at what they were telling me. I couldn't understand any of it -- was part of a prisoner's rehabilitation plan to remove all triggers before they had a chance to gauge his reaction to them, to see how he would

150

deal with things? But they were adamant, I was not allowed to read those beginning sentences of my impact statement at the panel hearing. However, they let those sentences stand, complete as I wrote them, as part of the full written impact statement that went into Terry Porter's file, which he and the panelists that day would be able to read. This would be just the start of many things that the Parole Board did that would not make any sense to me.

I actually mailed two impact statements that week to the Parole Board. Not long before my sister passed away, she reminded me of a letter. I knew, of course, which one she meant. About a year after Terry Porter killed our father, she penned a hand-written letter, in the form of a song, about her feelings. She was very musical and writing a letter like she did would have been a natural way for her to express herself. After a little digging, I found it and read my sister's words from all those years before, and it was easy to feel the rawness of her pain and the depth of the loss of her father. I wrote a note to the parole board explaining that my sister had passed away but she wrote this letter in 1992. I would appreciate it if they would put it in the Offender's file and include it as her Victim Impact statement.

Well, no, came the phone call, they were unable to include it. Why not? She can no longer be contacted, I was told, so they couldn't verify that she wrote the letter. And as well, they objected to one line she wrote: she had written that she felt that

John Terrance Porter belonged in a six-foot hole. This sentiment, and those words, the Parole Board found objectionable and didn't want included in a file.

By this point I was furious. Of course, I told them, she can't be contacted, she has passed away. When she wrote the letter, I continued, there was no place that she could send it to, not at that time, and we were not made aware in the years to come that letters could even be sent anywhere. So when the time came and I found out about the Parole Board and that they did indeed accept letters, I sent it in. And about that line, well, yes, I agreed with my sister, he did belong in a six-foot hole, and I could verify those were her feelings at the time, and would still be, I was sure, if she were alive today.

The Parole Board called me a few weeks later on what was the last day before their offices were closing for the Christmas and New Year break. Yes, they decided, they would include her letter in Terry Porter's file. I was very pleased, overjoyed really, because I knew, by law, the panelists for the upcoming hearing and all panelists at future hearings would have to read everything in that file and every letter. Best of all, so would Terry Porter. He would be able to read, in her own handwriting, what my big sister thought of him.

Merry Christmas, Deb.

Chapter 11 ~ Anchors

I met my friend Kim at work and we quickly became fast friends and would often see each other outside of work on a regular basis. Sound and non-judgmental, I came to rely on her and her opinion about so many things. And she could make me laugh, which was a valuable asset in any friend. I would come to tell her about what happened to my Dad all those years ago, in full detail, and all about what was going on with the Parole Board and what seemed to be my day-to-day frustration with them and all the things I was learning. I said to her that I should quit my day job and write a book: The Parole Board for Dummies. Or another working title that was a favourite of mine: Parole Board 101. I was joking around, but really, I could have used a book like that, and if I could find one at the local bookstore or Chapters, I would have bought it. I would have bought two copies, actually, highlight all the good parts and send one of them to the Parole Board so they could reference it if they needed any help. I found the Parole Board people on the surface to be as helpful as they could be; but as I pushed harder and asked more questions, I found some of their answers lacking basic common sense. And there was not just one person that I dealt with there; I spoke to many people. And different people would give me different answers to my questions so at times I found things to be quite confusing. I wished I had a road map of someone else's journey so I could see what route they had taken. I didn't need it all laid out neatly for me, as everyone has different experiences and different interactions with people, but at times I was overwhelmed by the information I was being told. However, I felt that the Parole Board hadn't had anyone ask them the tough questions as I was doing or present different situations to them either. In the end, I made it through, though, but I would still snap up a copy of Parole Board for Dummies if it were available. Maybe this is even an early template for it.

Over the years, most people who knew me didn't know what had happened to my father. And by most people, I mean friends of mine, people I worked with or people I would see every day. Yes, they might know he had passed away, but that was as far as it would get; that wall that I had built years before was still standing as I just found it easier to keep everyone at arm's length. Kim was the exception, though, and to her I would tell the whole story. To others, I would tell a little bit of what happened, but not a lot. Because why would I? I didn't want that part of my life to be the first thing people knew about me, or the last thing they remembered about me. And that was the same in regards to my Dad; his life was so much more important than his death was, and to me it was imperative that it continue to be. And I found that I

154

just didn't want to talk about it, so unless you happened to know me when my father was murdered, unless you were a part of my life at that time, chances were that you would have no idea. So as this was all unfolding, it would come as a huge surprise to a lot of people. When my colleagues at work found out about my story, they gave me unconditional support and they were willing to help me in any way they could. As I mentioned, my parents knew a lot of people, and some of them would eventually come to live in the Long-Term Care facility where I worked. I was worried what they would think and what their families would say.

I was told, however, that I was not allowed to mention it at work, not to talk to my co-workers about it, or discuss it with the people I looked after, even though I knew they would likely read about me and my family in the press. So when the media coverage broadened with local newspapers, radio and television picking up the story, when residents and their families saw what was happening and what I was going through, they were very upset. The depth of keeping things to myself even extended to my husband as he had no idea about the details of it all. He only knew the basics: that my father had been murdered a long time before and I had tried to move on as best I could. Details, though, he didn't know them and didn't press for them; he just trusted when the time was right I would tell him. And when I finally did, I am sure there were times through all of this that he must have felt like he was dropped in the middle of a nightmare.

But the people who did know me at the time of Dad's murder, the people who were the closest to me then, I am still friends with to this day. We may not be close geographically, but that has never mattered, and in true friendship it shouldn't. They have seen a special part of me that not many people in my life now, no matter how close they get, could ever see. They knew me before. My friends are a connection to my then self that I would never want to lose.

I've always said, surround yourself with good people and you will never go wrong, they will help steady you when you wobble and help you find your footing again. So, on my last night at work before I was to take some time off to go to Kingston for the Panel Hearing, Kim and I were outside. Our shift had ended at least forty minutes before and it was now close to midnight, and we were outside leaning against the railing on this clear and still January night. It was freezing cold out, but it didn't matter. She let me talk. I am worried, I told her, that I might change after this, that by revisiting the past I'll be affected so much that I won't be able to find myself again. I am worried about losing myself, my happy self, my crazy, life-loving self, my smiling, laughing self. Over the last few months, I could feel that part of me slipping away and she could see it too. What if, Kim, who I am and who others think I am has all been a mask and now it's going to be pulled off? What if, by exposing so much of myself lately, that I won't be able to get back to where I was? I didn't want to think that I was some sort of fraud to myself and to everyone around me for all these years.

You know, Lisa, she said, you will get through this. And at the other side of it, you will come out the stronger for it.

Chapter 12 ~ Batten Down the Hatches

The day before the panel hearing, Nick and I caught a VIA rail train to Kingston. Everything was sorted; our friend Donna would stay the night and make sure the girls got off to school the next day. We would be staying in a hotel overnight, attending the hearing in the morning, and then leaving late the next afternoon for home. I didn't have a whole lot to say on the two-hour trip that would take us west to Toronto, then onward to Kingston which was about the halfway mark between Toronto and Montreal. Leaning my head against the window of the train, I watched the blur of the wintry landscape of southern Ontario whiz past me. Friends have told me what a lovely place Kingston is: steeped in history, picturesque with beautiful limestone buildings and historical properties, and it sounded just like the kind of place I would normally love to visit. As well, Kingston is home to Queens University, St. Lawrence College and the Royal Military College of Canada. Kingston is a prison town also as it has the largest concentration of federal correctional facilities in Canada.

Glancing out the window, I thought back at all that had transpired in the few months since I received the first letter from the Parole Board that

October day. Raking up all the memories from the past disturbed the cobwebs on a box that I had put away in the back of my mind a long time ago. It was up high, on the top shelf in my mind, pushed right to the back, so it would be very hard to get at. Years ago, when I put it up there, a part of my mind had written across it, DO NOT OPEN. Do not open, because it will hurt you too much if you do. As the years passed, other things got in the way of the box, other things cluttered up the area. So here it was, almost twenty-one years later, and I had reached up and got that box off the shelf, opened it up a bit and peeked inside. I only hoped that I would be able to get the lid back on it again when I needed to.

At the hotel, I kept waking up through the night, thinking about what would come in the morning. I would drift fitfully in and out of sleep, but when it was time to get up and get the day started, my mind was clear. I was nervous but I was as ready as I was going to be. The front desk called us a cab to take us to Frontenac Institution, which they told us was about a ten-minute ride away from the hotel. I didn't bring much with me, just a pen and a notebook and the Victim Impact Statement that I wrote. There was something else that I had with me, though, something of my father's. I wanted to bring something of my Dad's because I still reasoned that this hearing was about him, not just about Terry Porter. Of course, I had been instructed that I wasn't allowed to bring photos and mementos to the hearing, but I really wanted to have something with me that would have a connection to my Dad. I had to think of what I could bring but at the same time not have it noticed and run the risk of it being confiscated or be told to put it away.

So in the days before we left for Kingston, I had a root around. When my sister died, a lot of my Dad's belongings that she had came to me. Actually, a lot of everyone's things have come my way over the years, and I am glad that they found their way to me. I have my Nana's jewelry box that is full of odds and ends, bits of her jewelry and an old perfume bottle of hers with traces of Chanel No 5 left in it. I have ninety-year-old handwritten letters that my Grandfather Slingerland wrote to my Grandmother before they were even married. And I treasure my Dad's old tin box of postcards that he sent home to his mother as he sailed the world during his Navy days. I like to have a look through all these things at times, to sit down and sift through all these memories that belonged to other people, touch the things their hands touched and then tucked away somewhere for safekeeping. It is all safe with me, my long ago family, and I cherish every one and count them amongst my most prized possessions.

I find what I am looking for tucked away in the Manual of Seamanship, Volume 1, 1951. It's another one of my treasures, my Dad's Navy book, and inside its front cover, he inscribed the names of the ships he sailed on, dated and then signed it. In the pages of the book, there is a black silk ribbon that at one time was tied around the base of my Dad's sailor hat. Despite the passage of time, you can still read H.M.C.S. Labrador on it; the gold letters stamped there many years before have not faded at all. I asked Nick to fasten a bit of velcro on the ends of it, to make it adjustable so it could fit my wrist like a bracelet; but when I was finished with it, it could be easily restored to its full length and returned to the book. So I was ready; I would have a bit of my father with me at the panel hearing. And with that black piece of silk ribbon secured around my wrist, it was almost like Dad was with me again and holding my hand through it all.

I can't even recall what the prison looked like. I just remember that it was a bitterly cold day with lots of snow underfoot when we stepped from the cab and walked up the steps into the building. There was a security section set up much like the screening area at an airport, and I showed them my identification and the letter that I was instructed to bring with me. Everyday events were happening around me: people were cleaning windows, emptying bins, shoveling snow from the steps and the front walk. It was only later that I realized that these weren't ordinary workers, they were inmates from the prison doing these tasks. Not the chain gangs of my imagination, no prisoners in handcuffs, shackled and wearing striped uniforms, but men who looked like everyday people in what looked to be everyday clothes. And, I realized, any one of

161

them could have got into the taxi we just got out of and been gone. So this was what minimum security in Canada was all about, I surmised. At least, I thought sarcastically, Nick and I were secure, as we were cleared and asked to stand off to the side and told that someone would be with us shortly.

I might not remember much about the outside of Frontenac prison, but I will never forget what the inside of it looked like. As we waited for someone to come and get us, I took a look around me and noticed that there were decorations for Valentine's Day hanging up everywhere. I had never been in a prison before, and I didn't really know what to expect, but even with the vast imagination that I had, I never thought that I would see cut outs of red hearts and cupids hung on the walls. And, I realized, they looked like the same ones that were hung up in the nursing home in which I worked. We had a great activity team who did their best to make the place look home-like and less institutionalized. I guess Frontenac Institution had the same thought in mind. Maybe they even had an activity team? And, I wondered, if I looked hard enough, would I find a framed Prisoner Rights Certificate similar to the Residents Rights Declaration that we had at work? I nudged Nick and pointed the walls out to him and asked what he thought about the hearts and cupids with bows and arrows in the front lobby of a prison. He was surprised as well but said to just try to forget about it for now, that there was no point in getting all riled up about decorations when I hadn't even made it up to the hearing room. Save your energy for that, he told me.

I felt as if I had a lead weight in my stomach as we waited, but it wasn't too long before the Regional Communications Officer came to greet us. We made small talk as she took us up to have a look at the room in which the Panel Hearing was going to be held. She showed me where my seat was and where I would stand to read my statement. She led us to a smaller room down the hall to wait and told us that she would come back and get us when they were ready. There was a wing chair on the far side of the room, and I dragged it over closer to the window, sat on the arm of it and looked outside. I didn't want to talk to anyone and I didn't want anyone to speak to me. I just wanted to be alone with my thoughts and to try to prepare myself. Prepare myself to read my Impact Statement, prepare myself for the emotions that would come with doing so, and to prepare myself to be in the same room as my father's killer.

Nick and I were led back to the average-sized meeting room that had tables set up in a rectangular formation and we were seated. At the table I was sitting at, my chair was just a slight bit ahead of the other people beside me, I was slightly forward of them and they were flanking me. I recall this distinctly because, to speak to Nick properly, I had to turn myself slightly and look behind me. To my right at the table was Nick and to his right was a Communications Officer. To my left was the

Communication Officer who was my primary contact at the Parole Board, and there was another officer beside her. There was a Guard standing in the corner at the far side of the room, and seated at the table in front of him was Terry Porter's Parole Officer and Terry Porter's assistant. Sitting across from the three of them were the two panelists, one male, one female; they were both lawyers, and they would conduct the hearing.

And sitting directly across from the panelists was the man who murdered my father.

I could not take my eyes off of Terry Porter. Here was the man who so violently killed my father, who wreaked havoc on our lives. Here was the man who haunted my dreams for years and whose name I could hardly say without spitting it out. I looked at his hands and thought of the life he took with them. I looked at his arms and thought of the struggle my father must have put up against them before he was overpowered. The only time during that hearing that my eyes would leave Terry Porter would be when I would glance down at my paper when I was reading my statement.

He would not look at me once.

The man who lived in my mind as a monster, an axe-murdering maniac looked very different compared to when I last saw him in court two decades before. Something astonishing had happened over the years: he became human looking. He was, I was sure, still the monster inside that I knew him to be, but this man sitting at the table did not look like a monster. He looked like a normal everyday person. If I saw him walking down the street, I would not look twice at him, there was nothing in his demeanor that would draw any attention to him, if he was in the line at Tim Horton's in front of me, he wouldn't look out of place. And that scared me even more than what my mind held him to be all through the years: the very ordinariness of him terrified me.

The panelists then introduced themselves and stated their roles within the Parole Board of Canada. It was clear from the beginning that the male lawyer was taking the lead in things. Introductions continued of the other people who were in the panel room: parole officers, communication officers, a lone guard. Then the male lawyer said that he would like to introduce Lisa Freeman, the Victim's daughter. I was stunned. I could not believe that a lawyer had just introduced me by my full name to the man who murdered my father. I wrote something in the notebook that I had in front of me and I turned slightly to my right to show my husband what I had written:"I cannot believe he just said my name!"

Normally, in any other situation, in any other setting, I would have said something, right then and right there. There would have been no chance that I wouldn't have. I felt that in this environment, though, I could not. This was, in my eyes, a very controlled one. The only opportunity I would get to speak in the panel room that morning was when I would read my pre-scripted words in the form of my already-approved-by-the-Parole-Board Victim Impact Statement.

I wasn't to deviate from that, I knew that, I had been told that. So on that morning, the Parole Board of Canada already knew what I was going to say. The problem was, though, that I had no idea what they were going to say.

So I sat there still and quiet. For the moment, there was something else to hold my interest, something else that pushed the ineptitude of this lawyer to another part of my mind. The discussion was about Escorted Temporary Absences that are part of Terry Porter's AA plan. He would like to be able to go to someplace called Hope House in Ottawa. His parole officer is talking about him, he's a low risk, she says, and then his assistant is speaking positively on Terry Porter's behalf as well. The time now comes for the lawyers to ask Terry Porter about himself, his time in incarceration and about his past.

I pick up my pen.

He is asked, this man, about his childhood. He looks straight ahead at the panelists, looking directly at them, and he is soft spoken when answering. He found out that he was adopted when he was five or six years old and he is 'shocked' at this. He had trouble with school, English being his worst subject. He would start substance abuse at 12 or 13 years of age. He started drinking at dances on the weekend, with his drug use progressing every

166

day. He left school somewhere in between grades seven and eight and found a job at a garage working in the muffler shop.

His progression of drug use, he continued, started with marijuana, but he would try other drugs too, mainly hash and Valium. He started injecting speed at the age of 17 in Cape Breton, Nova Scotia. He went on to say that starting at age 16, he had problems with the law. "It's not documented" but he was busted for selling marijuana, spending everything on drugs and alcohol. He had a few convictions for drug offences during the next few years.

The next conviction was in 1979 for assault with intent to wound. It was a two-staged attack that he carried out on his adoptive father. Terry Porter, when asked by the panelist for the details, told them that his parents were afraid of him. His father told him that "he was no longer welcome here" in regards to the family home. His mother and father were so frightened of him they barricaded themselves inside the house, but Terry Porter broke through a basement window and attacked his father. "When he wouldn't let me in, I broke in." he told the panelists. Terry Porter beat up his father so badly that he needed medical attention, and when he was at the hospital receiving it, Terry Porter followed him there to continue his attack. He stabbed his father in the emergency room puncturing his lung. He then continued to tell the panel that he was incarcerated for four years for that

167

crime and that, during that time, he was in and out of mandatory supervision.

Terry Porter went on to give details of his violent history. In 1983 he was in a psychiatric hospital in Dartmouth, Nova Scotia. He had been there for ten days, being admitted for a Valium overdose. He then said, "I went psychotic" kicking and attacking an orderly, kicking him in the ribs and facial areas, but starting the attack from behind.

He went on to say that he was put in St. John's medical hospital but he escaped from there. Then he was sent to a psychiatric centre in Abbottsford, British Columbia. Terry Porter then said that he lied about his mental health, and he lied about it to be in a psychiatric hospital instead of a prison. Because, he said, a "psychiatric hospital is like a Holiday Inn compared to prison."

Now where had I heard that before? Of course. Greg O'Driscoll had challenged Terry Porter all those years ago at the trial with those very words. Medical records from various psychiatric facilities across Canada showed that Terry Porter was admitted and discharged eleven times since the age of 17. Greg O'Driscoll suggested to Terry Porter on the witness stand that he was faking his psychiatric symptoms over the years in order to be admitted to psychiatric facilities to do 'easy time' instead of more difficult custodial time in a prison setting. In 1991 under oath, Terry Porter denied it. Twenty-one years later, Greg was proved right when Terry Porter admitted it.

168

My mind was overflowing with all this information. He was a liar and admitted it. Before he killed my father, he had a very violent past. He savagely beat, assaulted, intimidated, frightened, kicked and stabbed people – including his own father. He went on that morning to tell how he assaulted a taxi driver in 1986 by saying that he "punched and booted him when he was down." Then he was charged with forcible confinement of a girl he was seeing out west. Terry Porter told the panelist that he "was jealous and controlling, as well as physically and verbally abusive." When he was asked what happened that day, he said "She wanted me removed from the house, so I smashed the door in and grabbed her, put her in a car, struck her about the head, causing damage." I don't know what the panelists thought about him, but it was very clear to me that Terry Porter was a liar, a bully, and a jealous and controlling man. He knew the system and he played it well. He was a master manipulator who was able to fake symptoms and compliance to make life easier for one person: himself.

It was now time for the panelists to ask Terry Porter about the murder of my father. I was seated not twelve feet from the man who butchered him, and I could feel the bile rising in my throat. Surely to God he won't say anything that I didn't already know. I braced myself. And I put my pen down. Terry Porter had my full attention.

Mr. Slingerland, he said, was a nice man

who did not deserve to die. He said that he was lying on the witness stand when he said that he had blacked out, but he actually remembered it all. He had been drinking before he went in to see my Dad that evening but said he was still sober enough to drive. He went to the Brock Street property looking for his girlfriend, leaving his car running outside. He said he remembers "breaking Slinger's arm" but "couldn't remember using a weapon." He admitted that he was lying when he said that he couldn't remember attacking him and that when he was caught, he had fallen asleep in his car covered in Slinger's blood. It made me sick to hear him say my father's name. How dare he. How dare he sit there, speaking as if he really knew my Dad at all, and talk about him in such a casual manner, as if they were friends. He may have taken my Dad's life but he knew nothing about the life he took. I wanted him to shut up, not to talk about my Dad with such familiarity. DO NOT SAY HIS NAME AGAIN.

Terry Porter then said that after beating my father, he laid him on his side so he wouldn't choke.

'You liar,' I was screaming in my head as he spoke.

You did not lay him on his side, you son of a bitch.

Dad was found FACE DOWN.

CHOKE? YOU WERE WORRIED ABOUT HIM CHOKING?

CHOKING?

You fractured every facial feature he had.

But you were worried about him choking?

I really don't know how I kept my mouth shut in that panel room that morning. I should have just gone for broke and started screaming what was going through my head, and then get up and crawl over the table and start beating on him with my fists until they bled and they had to pull me off him.

But, of course, I didn't. Despite all I had heard that morning, I managed to keep it together and maintain my composure. I thought about Deb's letter that was in the panelist's file, and I knew that by this point Terry Porter would have already read her words. Now it was my turn and I stood up, took a deep breath and began to read mine.

"I didn't lose my father; he was taken from me. And I have been waiting almost 21 years for this day. I am here not only speaking for myself, but for every member of the Slingerland family, and for everyone who was touched by this tragedy. Through the years I've been haunted by not being there for my Dad during his final moments, as he lay alone, dying in the snow on a cold winter's evening in February 1991. But I'm here for him now.

Thank you, Panelists, for giving me this opportunity to speak.

I am one of Mr. Slingerland's three daughters. And 21 years may seem like a long time ago, but the passage of time has not diminished our grief. The impact that my father's murder has had on our family has been monumental, and we still feel it to this day. And to try to compose a Victim

Impact Statement that can adequately relay my grief is next to impossible. These words are the hardest I've ever had to write, and they are written with a strange sense of displacement; it is as if time has rippled. My mind is in a battle, trying to trick me into thinking this murder happened just days ago, not 20 years ago. To say that I feel re-victimized again is a gross understatement.

My older sister took our Dad's death especially hard. Eight weeks before his murder, she was diagnosed with cancer, so not only did she have her own burden to bear, she had the additional strain and stress of the murder of her beloved father to cope with at an already trying time in her life. She took the loss of our father with her to her own grave ten years ago, and she made me promise, when the opportunity came, to speak of her pain and the depth of her grief. She was a compassionate and forgiving person, but with one exception: in regards to the man who took her father from her, she was fervent in the belief that he should never be free again.

To this day, my younger sister cannot have anyone say the word 'Dad' to her without her falling apart. Anything connected to him, even the good things and the good times we shared, she dissolves in tears. Dad's murder shrouded her in a black veil that has never fully lifted. Her mental stability shifted for the worse after our father's murder, and that's with us trying to shield the worst of the horrors from her. Terry Porter has given her a life of anxiety and paranoia, and even now, almost 21 years later, she sleeps with a knife under her pillow to protect herself from the man who killed her Dad. And this is what she is like with Terry Porter behind bars. I dread to think what she would be like with him free.

As for myself, that evening all those years ago changed my life, forever altering my dreams and painting my nightmares red. The last image I have of my Dad is not of the quiet, hardworking man who loved fishing and telling of his adventures from his Navy days. Instead, I see what was left of him on a gurney in the hospital morgue, hacked away beyond recognition. Instantly, I am in that room again, being told by a Police Officer that I can't touch my Dad, that he is evidence now. This image is the fabric of the re-occurring nightmares that I have had over the years. Nightmares that aren't just contained to nighttime, but nightmares that seep into the reality of the here and now of my life. Terry Porter's actions have infringed on every moment of my life. The happy occasions like graduation, marriage and children have been duly celebrated, but marred as well by the absence of my Dad during these times. I try to keep my father alive for my children, telling them how much he would've loved to have met them and to be a part of their lives. How do you tell a child that their Grandfather was murdered? You don't, you just tell them that a bad man took him away, and hope, as the years go by, that they don't ask too many questions. You teach them right from wrong, but most of all you tell them that monsters don't hide under the bed, they walk amongst us. So you see, dear Panelists, this never ends, never ever ends. Terry Porter not only changed my perception of the world, but also of the people who live in it.

I have been tormented through the years with the knowledge that my Dad died alone, with no one there to reassure him, however misguided, that he would be okay and that help was on the way. By not being there to help him in his final moments that I have let him down in some way. Ridiculous, I know, but that is the one thing about tragedy: you forever live in that moment and try to make peace with the 'what-ifs' that float around in your head. And still, even 20 years later, I've not been successful in doing this.

Terry Porter is a man devoid of compassion, a killer who does not deserve Escorted Temporary Absences, Day Parole, or God forbid, Full Parole. Society, as a whole, and for its own safety, does not need people like him amongst us. I understand that they are community assessment tools that are used to determine the response of people living in certain areas to gauge their feelings about having offenders 'reintegrated' and 'rehabilitated' into their communities. Let me save you some time. Remorseless killers rate right up there with Pedophiles that everyday people don't want around them.

Why should compassion be granted to Terry

Porter? Well, I suppose there are those who say he's spent a lot of time in jail, let's give him a chance. No way. Why should he get anything he asks for? He's killed a man. He was interrupted twice during the brutal attack on my father. The first time he told the person to mind his own business and that it was none of his affair. The second time he was interrupted, Terry Porter went outside, came back in and dragged my Dad outside to continue his assault though my Dad pleaded with him to stop. There was plenty of time for Porter to show some compassion to my father, to show him some mercy, and to listen to his pleas. But he didn't. He is a man without a moral compass. Why should his life and his rights be worth more now than my father's did then?

In conclusion. I ask that the Parole Board review all material available in trial transcripts very carefully, paying particular attention to the extent and severity of Terry Porter's prior involvement in psychiatric institutions.

I ask the Parole Board to review ALL psychiatric records since Terry Porter has been incarcerated for this crime, the murder of my father.

I make the Panel aware that Terry Porter has a history of deception and manipulation in regards to his mental illness and that trial transcripts will reveal inherent tendencies.

I ask that the Panel review the documented opinions of various medical personnel that Terry Porter has a history of malingering, or faking mental illness.

I ask that the Panel be aware that Terry Porter has a history of escalating violence, which includes a serious attack on his own father. I am fearful for my own safety and for that of my family. I am fearful for any community that he finds himself in. Past documentation has shown time and time again that REHABILITATION DOES NOT WORK FOR THIS MAN. Don't be conned into thinking otherwise.

I make the Panel aware that Terry Porter has a history of violent UNPREDICTABLE behaviour, and a documented history of non-compliance.

Any one of these risk factors should be enough to keep Terry Porter behind bars for the rest of his life. The COMBINATION of all these risk factors makes him a high risk to re-offend with violent consequences. I feel that the National Parole Board would be negligent if they did not review the files and transcripts from the trial. I cannot stress this enough.

And who am I to make these recommendations to the Parole Board?

I am someone who has seen John Terrance Porter's handiwork first hand. I have seen his rage and his anger. Over nothing, really, my Dad simply did not know the answer to the question Terry Porter asked him. God help us all if someone or something were to really make him angry."

When I was finished reading, I was leaning against the table for support. But I did it. I stood in front of my Dad's killer, and in a strong and clear voice, I told him to the best of my ability what his crime did to me, to all of us. He didn't look at me once, but I made damn sure he heard me.

The last word went to Terry Porter. He said that he thought of Slinger's family through the years, "at Christmas and times like that", and he then mumbled an apology.

Look at me, you bastard, if you are sorry, look at me, let me see if it is in your eyes, in your face.

Terry Porter did not look at me.

The male panelist then asked Terry Porter that 'if the person you are now was cornered by your former self, how would your now self react to that?'

Terry Porter replied that 'he would call his AA person for support.'

The panelist had one more question. " When you look at yourself in the mirror, do you think of yourself as a murderer?'

Terry Porter paused…. Then answered yes.

To me, that pause was the most important thing that wasn't said that morning.

The panelist looked through the papers in front of him and said that there was nothing else in the file.

THERE IS NOTHING ELSE IN THAT FILE BECAUSE WE DID NOT KNOW THAT WE COULD SUBMIT THINGS! WE DIDN'T KNOW! I PUT THAT ON THE TOP OF MY VICTIM IMPACT STATEMENT BUT YOU SAID I

177

COULDN'T READ IT.

It was finished. We left the panel room and went back to wait in the room down the hall. I sat on the arm of that chair again and looked out the window. There was a snowstorm whipping up outside, and that is what my mind felt like. Everything I heard, and all the emotions I felt, were whirling around in my head. I was told that there would be a decision soon whether the Parole Board would grant Terry Porter the Escorted Temporary Absences that he was requesting. Just stop talking to me, I thought to myself, just let me sit here and look out the window. I could feel myself closing down, retreating, but I couldn't help it – my default settings were preset decades before.

They came and got us and we filed back into the room, and back to our seats. The male panelist thanked everyone for their input at today's hearing. He then went on to say "Thank you to Lisa Freeman for reading her Victim Impact Statement." This man did not just say my name again, I thought to myself. What is wrong with him? So not once, but twice, the same panelist said my name in front of Terry Porter. I knew, of course, that Terry Porter would read my name. It was signed at the bottom of my impact statement, by law I had to sign it, it had to be there. But no one, not once ever said that I would have my name spoken in front of Terry Porter. That was a whole new kind of violation. And, for God's sake, we weren't at a cocktail party; we were at a Parole Board of Canada Panel Hearing. For the man who axed my father to death. There was something very, very wrong with this.

I tried to focus on what they were saying. Yes, the panelists felt that the risk was low enough for Terry Porter to be escorted by his assistant and a mental health nurse to Hope House in Ottawa as part of his ongoing AA treatment. I thought that my head was going to explode. The risk was low enough! And what? There were no places in Kingston that he could go to? Nothing like a tax-payer funded field trip to Ottawa for how long? for the duration of up to eight hours? How many times did they say he was going there, ten times? And who's going with him? A nurse and an assistant, but no guard accompanying them? My mind was in a whirlwind, whipped up and fueled by disbelief and rage.

I was furious and I just wanted to get out of there. Back we went to the room, with the chair and the window and my coat. The communication officer tried to talk to me, but I screamed at her. I shouted and screamed at her and took out all my frustration about everything in an uncharacteristic outburst of rage and torrent of abuse. And when I was finished, I apologized to her. She didn't take it personally, she said, it was part of her job. She would put all what was decided in a letter and send it to me. Okay, yes, thank you.

I can't believe they didn't escort me out of the building after that. We got our coats, and she took us downstairs, back to security, and we picked

179

up our cell phones that we handed in when we first came in. Nick asked them to call us a cab. As we were standing there waiting, I saw Terry Porter's assistant outside speaking to someone. I pointed him out to Nick, and for a moment, a fleeting moment, I was thinking of going outside to confront him, to tell him not to be fooled by Terry Porter.

I had to restrain myself from doing so.

Thank God that cab came. Where to, he asked. Anywhere, just get me away from here.

By the time the cab dropped us off in downtown Kingston, I was finished being angry. Now the tears came. I can't remember the name of the restaurant in Kingston that we stumbled into that day, but I didn't want to go inside. I wanted to be outside. What I was feeling didn't want to be confined to a room where I couldn't let it out. I needed a vast emptiness so I could scream, let it out and have the wind pick it up and scatter it, and take my pain and spread it around so I alone didn't have to feel it. I knew there was a lake somewhere around here. Can't we just go there? It was about minus 15 with a snowstorm blowing in, and my face was a mess of frozen tears. No, we can't, Nick said, and got me inside and ordered me a hot drink. I didn't want food, but he ordered me something anyway. I was a wreck. I sat at that table and cried and sobbed and cried some more. There was no anger in me anymore; I got that out of my system back at the prison. Now all I could do was cry, not just a little bit; non-stop crying, the kind when you couldn't even speak you were crying so much. But I tried to talk, I was rambling on about my Dad, telling Nick all about him, how my Dad deserved better than this. That I had let him down, that I had let everyone down. I was lost in my own world of grief mixed with my anger at the decision of the panelists. It would be weeks later that Nick would tell me about that day in the restaurant and how he kept getting strange looks from people who were there and from other patrons at the tables around us. Even the waitresses going about their work and new customers coming in to wait for food to take out were giving him dirty looks and side glances. They would see a woman who was both angry and crying at the same time, with her voice raised, but in the next minute, so full of emotion that she couldn't even whisper enough words to string a sentence together. Nick figured that, judging by the looks he was getting that day, people likely assumed he was dumping me. We got back to the hotel, gathered up our things, and went back to the train station. The train heading back to Toronto was running late because of the snowstorm. I couldn't get out of Kingston fast enough. When we finally did board the train, I sat down in my seat exhausted and slept all the way home. Nick was probably very thankful that I did.

Chapter 13 ~ Sounding at Night

In the days and weeks after the panel hearing, frankly speaking, I thought that I was losing my mind. Life is full of road blocks and obstacles, and as a family, we had our fair share, but I've always been better able to see the problem, work on a solution, adjust and do my best to move on. Never meant that it was easy, or that it was something that happened quickly, but I was always pretty much able to deal with things. Not now, though. It wasn't for lack of trying, but this time there was just too much to cope with and too much for my mind to absorb.

Nightmares would plague me when I slept, but for the most part I was used to that. With my father's murder and all the horror associated with it, bad dreams were just what happened, and I wasn't surprised by them. I could be rattled by them and upset about them, but they just became a part of my life. At nighttime my mind was left to its own devices, and I really couldn't control what went on in there. But this time, after the Panel Hearing, it was what was happening during the daytime that had me concerned the most.

At any time, sudden and disturbing memories would float to the surface of my mind. This wasn't unusual in itself: just like anyone else, I could be busy and all of a sudden I would think of something, or someone. But what would worry me was that I was losing sight of being in the here and now reality of my life when this was happening. I didn't have to see anything to jar my mind about something, it would just happen and come on suddenly.

I was out one morning, doing the most routine of things; I stopped at the store to pick up a few groceries. I had a few basics, bread, fruit and then I stopped. I couldn't think of groceries any more. Out of nowhere, the predominant thought in my mind was that my Dad was dead. This was twenty-one years after his murder, and I was in the middle of the grocery store, and it was just as if I was finding out for the first time that something horrible had happened to my Dad. Worse still was that I couldn't shift that thought from my mind. I could feel tears pricking at my eyes, and then I could feel them on my face. What was I doing here buying bread? Dad was dead. I was so upset by this, I just put the few things I had in my hands down and left.

I got home and sat down. I don't know how much time had gone by, but I was finally back to what was currently happening, back to the here and now. I was shaken and scared, I had never lost control like that before. I always thought of myself as a very strong person and was regarded as so. Nick would come looking for me, and I would still be there, sitting on the arm of the chair, just looking out the window. He said it looked like I was waiting for someone. I probably was.

These flashbacks would happen for some time to come. They would never last very long, but when they came, it would be with such intensity and with so much feeling behind them. Unannounced would come the picture of my Dad, horribly injured but still alive. Just give us Dad back no matter what condition he was in, we would take care of him. As long as he was still alive. This same thought and the same picture was as if it were suspended in my mind and I couldn't push it out; it would have to dissolve away on its own. Not only was there the pain connected with the thoughts, there was a physical ache as well. The ache of wanting something so very badly and then the realization that there was nothing there to have.

Most disturbing though was when I would look at my five-year-old. I knew she was my daughter but, at the same time, she could have been someone else, and to my damaged mind, for a minute she was. She looked very much as I did when I was a child, and she had the same happy and laughing qualities that I did. Whatever was happening in my mind would make time blur: I would see her and then get a strange feeling that I was looking at a younger version of myself. I was sad for her, sad for this little girl, this little me. And scared of what she had to deal with as she got older. Soon, though, she was back to who she was. My mind would orientate to my surroundings and then, and then I would realize that it was only in my mind. All this not only upset me, but it terrified me as well.

Mixed in as well with this was anger and fear. The anger was explainable, and the anger was what I was so worried about surfacing again prior to the panel hearing. From the day I received the letter informing me about the Panel Hearing, I could feel the old anger coming back. It was mixed with fear, too, and that was something that I had not felt for a long time. Terry Porter was in prison and had been for quite some time. That made me feel safe. For years and years, I didn't know what he was up to, and really, I didn't need to know. He was in prison and that kept my fear of him locked away, too. Now though, he had been granted absences away from the prison. This was, the Parole Board told me, the first steps, the first baby steps towards full parole and re-integration into society.

So even though they were escorted trips from the prison, he would still be out of prison. I was having a lot of difficulty with that. Night time and sleep became an ordeal. I would fall asleep only to be wakened during the night by some noise in the house. Of course, it was just the house settling, as we lived in an older house where the floorboards seemed to take on a life of their own after dark.

But I would wake up, convinced that my Dad's killer was in the house. My heart would race and I would lay there trying to think of what to do. I was panic-stricken and I was afraid to open my eyes, afraid of what I would see, that tight coil of wire called fear wrapping itself around me. In the end, I would wake Nick up, and he would say, don't worry, it's just the house settling, and then I would eventually fall back to sleep. There were nights, though, when I would wake up terror-stricken and I would lay there clenching my fists and blankets and talk myself into being very still. I would count to ten and focus on the familiar sounds around me. Nick's breathing beside me, the sound of the ceiling fan whirring in the next room, the sound of the traffic from the street. There was no one there, I would tell myself a few times over, just breathe, breathe and try to fall back asleep.

And then there was the ongoing issue of the sliding door in our bedroom, which opened up to a very nice upper deck. I was never a huge fan of sliding doors because I would, of course, associate them with my Dad being dragged through one to the patio where he was killed. But things were different now. With hot summer days and warm summer nights, having that sliding door open was a reprieve to the heat and, when opened, there was a nice breeze that would blow in which made it easier to sleep. Not that spring or summer, though. I could not have it open, I refused to have it open and it was stifling hot. I couldn't have it open because then I would wake up in the night at the slightest noise from outside thinking that Terry Porter was out there on the deck. Unreasonable? Yes. Irrational? Yes. But not to me, and with the state my mind was in, it was logical. Terry Porter was out of prison.

He could be anywhere. We would go to sleep with it shut, and then when Nick knew for sure that I was soundly asleep, he would get up and open it and let the breeze circulate in the room again.

If I could have bricked the sliding door up and be done with it, I would have.

I think the hardest thing to explain is the effect of having my name said in front of Terry Porter at that Panel Hearing that day. If he didn't hear it the first time, he was sure to have heard it the second time the lawyer said it.

By law, Terry Porter has the right to know who is complaining about him. My right to my privacy does not come into it. My victim impact statement had to be signed. When things are submitted into an Offender's file, the locator details, like your address and contact numbers, are removed, but your name remains. I wasn't all right with this, and I am sure many other people who have found themselves in the same situation didn't like it either. The Parole Board was very clear though: names must be on statements.

Not once did anyone tell me that I was going to be introduced to the room. Nor did I need to be; in my Victim Impact Statement that I submitted a month beforehand, which the panelists read as part of the file clearly stated who I was: I was one of Roland Slingerland's three daughters. In my life and outside of that room, I was many things to many people: mother, daughter, friend, wife, employee, but that day and in that capacity, I was someone's daughter. And if I were asked, I would have said to introduce me as the Victim's daughter. Problem was, though, that no one asked me.

After I got home from Kingston, I could feel what having my name said in front of my Dad's killer that day took from me, what it stripped from me. Anonymity. Up until that point, to Terry Porter, I was a name on a sheet of paper. When my name was spoken in front of him, when he heard my name, I became someone. Whether or not he realized it really didn't matter. Because I did, I knew what happened. And by becoming someone to Terry Porter, I lost some of myself. I had already lost enough of myself to Terry Porter through his crime and not through any choice of my own, so I would never willingly give any of myself to him. But I didn't have to, someone else did. On that cold February morning at a prison in Kingston, Ontario, a piece of myself was taken from me and handed to Terry Porter. And for that, the blame lay fully on the Parole Board of Canada.

Terry Porter was always able to read my name on the statement in front of him. Now, since he heard my name, spoken out loud, in a setting in which I had no control, in my mind it became the fear of 'he knows my name.' And then the realization of 'he knows my name' because someone told him. And if someone told him my name, what else can he find out? What else could be told to him?

When you feel you have no control of a

188

situation and that decisions are made without your consent, to me that constitutes fear. I was in an environment that day in which I should have expected to feel protected. Yes, I knew that I would be in the same room as my father's killer. I knew that, and it was my choice to present my statement in person. That was my choice. I knew there were other options that I could have taken. No one gave me the option about my name, though. I told them who I was in my statement, the statement that they needed a month before so they could go over it. In that statement, I clearly wrote and just as clearly stated that day in the panel hearing I was fearful for my safety and for that of my family's. So that morning, the panelists, when not instructed otherwise, should have introduced me as one of Roland Slingerland's daughters, and really that is all anyone, especially Terry Porter, needed to know.

In my eyes, they were too occupied with making sure the Offender was comfortable in his mind on that day. In re-reading the Do Not list it certainly seems so. Do not address him directly. Do not threaten him. Do no use bad language in front of him. Do not bring in graphic pictures.

Do not forget about people like me, Parole Board.

Chapter 14 ~ Lost and Found Again

I continued to see the trauma nurse counselor and I told her just some of the things that were going on. I had always been able to just help myself through life, see my own way through, and I still was reluctant to tell someone fully what was happening. I liked her, we could talk, but I had only known her for a short time. Maybe that shouldn't have made a difference in things, but to me it did. The fortress wall I built up years before remained strong.

So I tried to keep on top of things as best I could. I was irritable, though, from the lack of sleep. Even though I would nap through the day, there were no unbroken consecutive hours of rest. And I would find myself losing my temper with the people who were closest to me, namely my family. I would snap at Nick over nothing because he couldn't give me answers I needed, couldn't steer me in the right direction of things because it was just too much out of his realm. Kayla was 14 at the time, and like most teenagers, she would push my buttons to try to rile me. I didn't take the bait. But now that was different; it seemed that she was purposely looking to upset me, to add to the burden of what I was already carrying. Looking back, she was just being a regular teenager and on the whole she was a good one. And on top of this, I was going to work which could be a stressful environment as well, and you never knew what kind of shift you were going to have. Some nights it was easy to be at work, and I could leave all the outside things happening in my life at the door. Other nights though, I couldn't. It was impossible to focus, impossible to put a fake smile on and interact with people easily.

I began clenching my teeth in my sleep, something that I had never done before. So that made my head hurt, and it would last for days. My neck and shoulders were stiff and sore as well. Not only was I clenching my teeth, I was also clenching my fists and scrunching my shoulders up to my ears when I slept. From fear or stress? Probably a combination of them both. The mental strain I was under was now taking its physical toll. I would cry a lot, sleep as much as I could, wherever I could fit it in. Sleeping brought little comfort, though, because of the dreams and fears about Terry Porter. It was a viscous circle that I could see no end to. And when the thought came into my head that if this was what the rest of my life was going to be like, that I didn't think that I wanted any part of this anymore, it scared me. Laughing, life-loving Lisa was reduced to this. I needed help. I was breaking down, I could see it, and I could feel it. I did not want to become another one of Terry Porter's victims, not ever, and certainly not after I had gotten through so much.

A week after getting back from the Panel Hearing in Kingston, I received a letter from

Correctional Services. Along with the Parole Board, I would also receive information about Terry Porter from Correctional Services Canada. Corrections fell under the umbrella of Public Safety Canada and also included under that umbrella were the Royal Canadian Mounted Police (RCMP), Canadian Security Intelligence Service (CSIS), Canada Border Services, as well the Parole Board of Canada. Correctional Services assigned me a Victim Services Officer that would provide me with any future decisions that may occur in regards to Terry Porter. The way I saw it, it was the Parole Board who made the decisions and Correctional Services who enforced them.

Terry Porter, the letter would tell me, was eligible for a judicial review, which is a decision to reduce the offender's parole ineligibility period. Offenders sentenced for a murder committed on or after December 2, 2011, will no longer be able to apply for a judicial review. However, offenders sentenced for murder before that date were still able to apply. Terry Porter killed my father in 1991, so he was eligible. A judicial review, the letter continued, does not grant parole to an offender, but it could reduce the period before which an offender can be considered for parole. The judicial review was better known in Canada as the 'faint hope clause.' And, just to make things more confusing, Correctional Services would only notify me if Terry Porter chooses not to apply.

It seemed to be one thing after another.

Shortly after being back from the panel hearing in which Terry Porter was granted temporary absences from the prison, at only the 21-year mark of his sentence, here is a letter from Corrections stating that now he was eligible for a shorter wait time between parole periods. Included in the letter as well was a section that calculated the eligibility dates for the various forms of parole for Terry Porter. When I first read it, I thought they had mixed the dates up: it said the month and day of his parole dates was 02-05, which was February 5th. That wasn't right, I thought, that's the date of my dad's death, the day that Terry Porter murdered him. I called to clarify, but what I was reading in the letter was correct. The eligibility dates were right, but it seemed very wrong to me that the date that Terry Porter's life would move on was the very same date that he killed my father. It seemed Terry Porter was given another birth date, a new birth date to celebrate when he would go forward with his life. Surely they could have come up with another date for Terry Porter's new lease on life, a day other than the date of my father's death, the date he murdered him. Again, that was just one of the many things that the Parole Board did that didn't make too much sense. Not to me anyway.

Something had to happen before I could think about all of this and even begin to try to wrap my head around it. Nick and I already had a talk between us to decide where to take all of this. Do we just leave it and let the process happen? Or do I

193

do what I can to make people aware of what powers the Parole Board has and what rights an offender has? After all, I hadn't spoken about this murder a lot in the intervening years. If I didn't say anything, no one would be any wiser, no one would know. But I would know, and that was the deal breaker. I couldn't just sit back knowing what the Parole Board could do to people, to know that the basic right of privacy was not applicable to anyone unless you were the Offender. So, on yet another cold winter evening, February again, it was time to tell the rest of the family what had been going on, and what could possibly happen in the near future, in regards to this review. So we gathered at my mother's house and there, as the winter night closed in around us, I told my mother, my Aunt, her husband and Caroline about everything. About being notified about the escorted temporary absences and the hearing that I went to, and I explained about the faint hope clause and the review that Terry Porter was now eligible for.

The very first thing that my mother and sister said was that the 25-year mark hadn't passed yet and that was part of the original sentence: Life Imprisonment with no parole for 25 years. Everyone in the room was surprised that anything was happening at this point, 21 years after the murder. I told about being named twice in front of Terry Porter, told them about his demeanor, what he looked like, and I told them about his lying on the stand all those years ago. I told them what I learned from the hearing about his past, and they were shocked that he had such an extensive record. I told them about my impact statement and getting Deb's letter from all those years ago in. We needed more, though, as many as we could get into that file. I told them that the first thing I was going to do was to contact the Parole Board and put in a complaint about the lawyer, and then we would work on things from there. Everyone supported me 100 percent and were fully behind me when I said I was going to try to do what I could to keep Terry Porter in jail as long as possible. Other members of the family would be writing their own statements into Terry Porter's file. News that things could be sent in and submitted to Terry Porter's file came as a surprise to them as well.

Never again, we vowed, would my Dad's file be so woefully empty.

There were two other people who had to be told about what was going on. One was 14 and the other was 5, and telling them would be one of the very hardest things I had to do. They were, of course, my daughters. The older one very likely knew that something was going on. I would race to grab the phone once I saw the words Parole Board on the call display, and I would shush her out of the room while I tried to speak to them. Since I last told her all those years ago that a bad man had taken her Grandpa Slinger away, nothing else was said about anything. The years went by and I didn't revisit the subject again. Yes, she would hear the stories that I would tell her, the good memories but as to the worst of things, we didn't discuss it at all. Since she had a cousin who was a year older, I am sure that they probably traded information as time went by, whatever snippets they heard over the years. Looking back, maybe I should have spoken to her earlier about things, but to my mind, I had a very good reason not to. So I sat her down one day and told her about the parole hearing, the outcome of it, and how things will eventually change in our future. I showed her the mock-up of the In Memoriam that was to be printed in a few days time, and that I really didn't know what to expect in regards to people's reaction from it. And as to what was going to happen in the future, I just didn't know. I only knew that I would continue to try to keep her Grandfather's killer behind bars as long as possible.

She said she didn't know how this would possibly affect her. My answer to that was quite simple: because she was my child, it had affected her since the day she was born. She just hadn't realized it yet.

The dining room table at our house has hosted a lot over the years, including many games of Monopoly, Scrabble, and multiple card games. It has been a gathering place for birthday parties, tea parties, and where we would all sit down for our family suppers, and where all the family would come and gather for many grand Christmas feasts over the years. Now though, Nick and I sat down at the table with our younger daughter to tell her what was happening. This, we knew, was going to be the hard one, because unlike her sister, she could only be told so much and she was not going to be exposed to it in the same way. Her older sister, of course, could read and knew her way around a computer, and she had a vast amount of people that she came in contact with on a daily basis who may or may not say anything to her. Not the little one, though, her life was mainly anchored to us, and life was more of what we exposed her to, not the other way around as in the case of her sister, who was out in the world. And I really didn't want to tell a five-year-old senior kindergarten student about the harshness of the world. So Nick and I had to choose our words carefully.

I say that, but really, all my words were only in my head. I could not get them out, could not get them into sentence formation. And when I would start to convert my thoughts into actual words, I found that I couldn't do it. They wouldn't come, they were stuck in my throat. I tried, but I was unable to speak, and with the racking sobs that came, I was unable to breathe. The weight of the horror, however watered down it was going to be, was locked inside of me. It came down to one thing: I did not want my children to know the horror of my past. I did not want my happy-go-lucky, just happy to be on the planet little five-year-old girl to know just how bad the world could be, and how closely it had touched her mother.

I sat with my head in my arms crying as

Nick told her. He touched on the very basic of information, only what she needed to know and nothing beyond that. She had a few questions, and he answered her truthfully. And then she put her arms around me, gave me a hug and said, don't worry, Mama, it'll be okay. And with those few words and with the resiliency that children have, I knew both my girls would be all right.

But I wasn't okay and I knew I had to get myself straightened out before I could go any further. I am very lucky to have a great doctor and to be not only in his care but also in the care of his nurse practitioner. Being under so much stress was finally taking its toll and with the latest about the judicial review coming so soon on the heels of the Panel Hearing, I could really feel that things were getting on top of me. So when I called my doctor's office to make an appointment, it was for the physical things I was going through: teeth clenching, headaches, fist clenching, shoulder and neck pain.

After I was showed into his office, I sat down in the chair, and my doctor came in and asked how I was doing, and I told him about all the physical pain that I was experiencing. And as I was talking, I started to cry. And then the whole story came out, haltingly; and between sobs, I condensed the murder, the parole board, the hearing I'd been to, the flashbacks, the nightmares and the fear, all put into rambling sentences that didn't sound like anything sensible to me. My doctor said that he was surprised that I had been his patient for all these years and he didn't know about any of this at all, not even the murder. And why didn't I come in earlier, he asked, if I could see that I was struggling and needed help? I told him that I just don't ask for help, hadn't ever before, and that I was strong and stubborn and that combination had prevented me from doing so.

He said that he would help me, even if it meant me coming into his office to sit there and cry and to talk things over with him. As for feeling weak about asking for help, he said, "Lisa, it is the strongest people who ask for help when they need it, that is where the strength is." And with that, my doctor and his nurse practitioner Monica helped put me back together again.

Surround yourself with good people and they will help steady you when you wobble. And they did.

The crying would ease up, not all of it, but the worst of it would subside. The flashbacks continued, but after time, they too stopped. I was still waking up in the night with my fists clenched, and still waking up thinking that Terry Porter was out there somewhere. I was angry, too. I was angry with the Parole Board of Canada. I was angry that they said my name in front of my Dad's killer, and I was angry because of what part of myself I lost by their actions. I tried telling myself that Terry Porter hadn't hurt my Dad for a long time and that I wouldn't let him hurt me either. But I struggled through the physical pain from sleeping poorly, sleeping with my body tensed up, and my head pounding from clenching my teeth in the night was wearing me down.

Anger can be a great motivator for some, and I called the Parole Board and spoke to the Communications Officer who was at the panel hearing that morning. I told her that I didn't think that I should have been introduced to Terry Porter when the lawyer started and finished the hearing. And anyway, I said, why would Terry Porter even need to know my name at all, written or spoken? Because, I was told, he has the right to know who is complaining about him.

I went quiet for a moment and let those words register. I asked her to repeat herself. Then I asked for the name of the person that I could make a direct complaint to.

I was given the name of the Regional Vice Chair of the Parole Board of Canada. Good, I had a person that I could start with. The first letter I sent outlining my complaint was January 22nd, 2012, less than ten days after the hearing. In response I received a phone call from the Regional Manager of Community Relations and Training. He confirmed with me that I already knew that the Offender would know my name because of my statement, submitted, as required, with my name on it. I assured him that in my many dealings with various communications officers prior to the panel hearing, I was not told that a panelist had the right to refer to me by full name in front of an offender. In our conversation he apologized for the 'communication error.' After the phone call with that manager, I received a letter from the regional director of the Parole Board, stating that the Board will, at times, not use the new name of a victim when expressly requested. The onus was on me to tell them how I would like to be addressed. Wrong, I countered, the onus was on the Parole Board of Canada to tell me that I would be introduced at all. Common sense dictates, I told them, that no-one who is participating at a panel hearing should be required to mention that he or she does not want to be introduced to the killer of their family member.

As well, I continued, the information was not relayed to me despite dealing with at least three different communications officers, and was not mentioned on any printed information that I had received from the Parole Board. I then stressed how imperative it is that this important information should be on the printed correspondence that is sent out to victims. And then I made another suggestion: perhaps someone should review their policy and procedures to ensure that 'communication errors' like this do not occur again.

Shortly afterwards, I received a letter in the mail from the Regional Director General and the Regional Vice Chair of the Parole Board. In it they stated that they regretted any discomfort that I experienced at the Panel Hearing in January 2012. Discomfort? Discomfort didn't even begin to describe what I experienced.

And the 'letter of regret', as I came to call it, didn't even come close to what I wanted. I've always said to my children that when you tell someone that you are sorry, that means that you will try not to do it again. The Parole Board wasn't willing to change things. These people, I concluded, just didn't get it. Letters of regret meant nothing to me. The sheer wrongness of the situation is what angered me. Letters were useless. I wanted change.

Chapter 15 ~ Even Keel

Every year I put a memorial in the local paper for either Dad or Deb. It was a little something I liked to do, and when Deb was alive we would split the cost for Dad's. Even if it wasn't his turn this year, I was going to put one in for my Dad. I wanted this one to be different from the regular memoriams of the past, but I needed to word it so it was still a record of his passing and our remembrance of him. After a few false starts, I liked what I had finally come up with. It started off about reaching the 21-year point of his death, and then I went on to list what his murderer, who was four years away from his parole eligibility date, was entitled to. In it, I made an appeal to people who may have known my Dad or our family, as well to the general public. And that if anyone reading this, and who agreed that this killer should be kept behind bars, please see my page and the pdf file so they too could send a personal letter of protest to the Parole Board.

As well, I needed help setting up that extra page on Facebook so I could post information there in an attempt to keep our far-flung relatives in Canada and friends up to date with what was happening. The perfect person to ask was my childhood friend, Tammy, who grew up beside me all those years before and still lived on the same street. I bundled myself up in my winter coat and gathered up all the papers and pictures that I had and walked the two blocks behind my house to hers. We sat down and I explained what I had in mind but that I didn't really know how to go about it. I brought her up to date about the parole board, panel hearing and everything that was going on and told her about Dad's memoriam and what I needed to pull it all together. So over the course of a few evenings, we came up with the Justice4dad title for the Facebook page, and together we set it up and found the right wording for a Letter of Protest that people could download from a pdf file directly from the Justice for Dad page, which they could fill out and send to the Parole Board to be included in Terry Porter's file. As the short winter days drew in around us, I looked at my childhood friend and thought about how another circle was forming in my life by working with her again. When we were nine or ten years old, we sat in this very same house, handwriting a community newsletter together, which we called the 'Gladstone Gazette.' Tammy and I went door to door selling copies and even went to the local shops in the neighbourhood to sell them advertising space! And now, all these years later, we were on Gladstone again, putting our heads together and working on yet another project.

I did a mock-up of the memoriam and sent it to the local newspaper and spoke to the person there who helped me with notices in the past. She read it over and checked for errors and then asked me what was going on, so I briefly filled her in. She told me she had to check with the legal department of the paper first to see if they could run it as she hadn't seen a memoriam like it before. I crossed my fingers that they would run it, but I had a back-up plan in case they didn't: I would simply insert it as a classified ad. But I was very glad when she called to say that, yes, they would indeed include it in the Memoriam section and it would run in the edition closest to the date of my father's death. As well, I was told, someone from the news department was going to contact me. My memoriam with a twist intrigued more than a few people, and it hadn't even been published yet.

The memoriam for my Dad published on the date of his passing including links to both my Justice for Dad page and the pdf file worked. The response I received was so much more than I expected. Even though my husband protested, I included my cell phone number in the ad, as well as my email address. I reasoned that if anyone who may have known my Dad from way back then, perhaps they might not have been computer savvy or have easy access to one. So I had to make sure that I was reachable to everyone, and I was glad that I did that. I had so many of my Dad's old friends contact me, telling me stories of my Dad and offering to write in statements for the Offender's file. People contacted me who remembered my parents from those long ago days, and they wanted to help out, too. The general public reached me

205

mainly through my email address and the Justice for Dad link. Regular everyday people were outraged that, even though they hadn't known my Dad, his murderer was eligible for so much, and well before the 25-year mark was reached in his life sentence. So I had many people reach out to me, many letters of protest went into the offender's file, and many, many people expressed their displeasure with the Parole Board and the fallacy of which Life Imprisonment in this country truly means.

In the meantime, I received notification from Correction Services Canada on March 30, 2012, stating that Terry Porter did not apply to have his period of parole ineligibility reduced within the time frame set out in Section 745 of the Criminal Code. The Offender, it read, has no further opportunity to apply for a judicial review.

This notice from them came approximately six weeks after the In Memoriam for my Dad appeared in the newspaper. How much weight did the subsequent Letters of Protests that went into his file carry in regards to his decision not to apply? That I will never know. What I did know was that I got a huge amount of satisfaction with the knowledge that I was doing something.

I looked across the dining room table at the man who was taking down notes as I spoke. Whom did he remind me of? Superman? No, that wasn't it. Ah, wait, yes, it was, but in his Clark Kent persona. I really didn't know this man, but I knew of him, as I often read his stories in our local newspaper. And now, on this miserably cold March morning, I was telling him mine. Jeff Mitchell was very easy to talk to as I led him through the story of the crime, the intervening years, the panel hearing and what happened that day. I described the Valentine-themed reception area of Frontenac Prison, and the words from the Parole Board that infuriated me, of how an Offender has the right to know who is complaining about them. I concluded with the memoriam that had appeared in his paper the month before.

He put his pen down, asked me a few questions while he absently gave our German Shepherd a few friendly pats. Whiskey had been at this reporter's side since he entered the house a few hours before and loved the random pats on the head that Jeff would give him in between his questions and note taking.

I knew I had surprised Jeff with the things I had told him when I wasn't too sure if I would. When I told most people what I had been going through, they were always surprised or shocked at the whole story. But Jeff was a seasoned reporter who had spent a lot of time in courtrooms, who had undoubtedly heard a lot and seen even more. He assured me, though, that my story was unusual.

But before we could continue, I had to send the dog out of the room. Instead of just sitting on the floor beside Jeff, he was now trying to paw his way up to him. Things were getting far too amorous, and I was trying to make a good impression, which was hard to do with Whiskey acting as if no one had ever paid him any attention before. So before a full-grown German Shepherd found a way to make it on to his new best friend's lap, I shooed him out of the room and shut the French doors behind him.

About ten minutes later, we were just wrapping things up when I heard it. It was an awful gnawing sound. I ignored it, thinking that it was likely some noise from the street. Jeff and I continued talking, and then I heard it again. What was that noise? It was louder and it sounded somewhat satisfied. I left Jeff for a moment while I went to investigate, and I found my answer close to the front door. There in front of me was a drooling, 75-pound German Shepherd with one of the reporter's leather shoes held between his paws. He had a very happy look on his face.

Needless to say, I was mortified. Whiskey had never done anything like this before, I told Jeff as I wiped down his wet shoe with a piece of paper towel. I assessed the damage: Whiskey had chewed some of the toe of the shoe away and gnawed a big hole into the side of it as well. I begged Jeff to let me pay for the shoes, but he wasn't having any of it.

Jeff Mitchell had the good grace not to make a run for the door, but instead he finished up the interview and thanked me for my time. He put what was left of his shoes on and reassured me again that I wasn't to worry about what had happened; it would make a great story to tell his colleagues.

Clark Kent? Superman? Yes, you are, Jeff, a

super nice man.

My story was told shortly after in our local newspaper and Jeff did a superb job. My mother approved of the story as well and liked Jeff's writing style. It was a brutal crime and my Dad had suffered horrific injuries, but Jeff didn't solely focus on that. In his writing, Jeff told our story and his readers about our Dad the person, not just as a murder victim. And as a family, we appreciated that. In his article, he included the links to my site through social media and more protest letters would make their way into Terry Porter's growing file in Kingston. The feedback from the public was about 99 percent in support of what I was doing. The other percentage didn't agree with me, saying that he had done his time and it was time for me to let it go and move on. And I was fine with that minority as everyone is entitled to their own opinion. But to those people I say, put yourself in my shoes and think about what you would do if it were a loved one from your family that this happened to. I didn't need people to like me, I didn't need to be popular, I had no ego to feed. What I was looking for was support, and that is exactly what I got. And from all the support I was receiving, it helped me in the process of dealing with things and to move forward. And, I would find, it was when I stopped moving that I struggled the most.

I am willing to bet that there are few people in Toronto and the Greater Toronto Area who don't know who Michele Mandel is. As a long-time writer with the Toronto Sun, she has traveled the world covering a variety of different assignments. Her articles bring clarity to the news, and her readers know she will tell it like it is. I have read her articles for many years, and her column currently deals with justice issues. She was just the person I needed, and it was my pleasure to meet with her one morning and to spend a few hours in her company talking about my Dad, my story and the obstacles that I was facing with the Parole Board. Just like Jeff Mitchell before her, and many reporters since, Michele was surprised when I told her my story and what challenges and hurdles I was dealing with. She took her notes, asked questions and made comments about the state of what life imprisonment in this country means and recorded a short video that her readers could access.

When our time together was finished, I thanked her and waved her off as she pulled out of my driveway. Then I headed back into the house to let Whiskey out of the basement. This time, and with this reporter, I was smart. When Michele had first come into the house I suggested that she leave her shoes on. And then, with a big dog treat in my hand, I lured Whiskey downstairs. I couldn't take the chance that, in the absence of her shoes, Whiskey would start sniffing around for another snack, just a little something to nibble on. I had visions of him eating a hole into her briefcase or chewing on her purse, so it was much easier to lure him completely out of Michele's (and her possessions) line of vision. Solution met.

In a Toronto Sun exclusive, my story was printed with the headline 'Life' Just a Cruel Joke, which summed up nicely the myth of what life in prison is in this country. My story was published shortly after the trial of Michael Rafferty and Terri McClintic where Rafferty had been convicted of first degree murder and sentenced to Life Imprisonment with no parole eligibility for twenty-five years. Rafferty abducted and murdered eight-year-old Victoria "Tori" Stafford from Woodstock Ontario. This little girl's disappearance and the subsequent search and investigation were widely followed across Canada. It was a truly heart-breaking story, and the public was glad of the conviction and the life sentence handed to Michael Rafferty. With my story following so quickly on his sentencing, it reminded people that a life sentence in Canada is not at all what it seems. Michele's well-written article told of the challenges I was facing with the parole board and the reality that parole starts at the 22-year mark, not the 25-year mark that is widely quoted. And it brought home the fact that Michael Rafferty would someday be entitled to accelerated parole just as Terry Porter had been. The story in the Toronto Sun hit an exposed nerve with an already fed up Canadian public that clearly still held the image of the sweet, smiling little girl that was murdered by a monster. A monster, who, in popular opinion, should be locked up and the key then thrown away. Not the case, my

211

story reminded people, not the case at all. The public is largely misinformed about the reality of what happens to prisoners after sentencing and long after the media headlines have faded. We all know of the Paul Bernardos, Michael Raffertys, Russell Williams and other high profile killers. But what about the killers who are lesser known to the public but whose crimes loom just as large to the families whose lives have forever been changed? These killers should remain behind bars as well. Truth in sentencing shouldn't be subjected to the interpretation of Corrections Canada officials -- life should mean life. And really, it shouldn't even come down to money and the cost of keeping prisoners locked away.

It should come down to justice.

My Dad's story and my continuing struggle with the Parole Board was gaining momentum and with any exposure I had, I would duly put it on my Justice for Dad page to keep it up to date. The Justice for Dad page that Tammy and I put together became a conduit for information. My family was widespread all over Canada from the East Coast to the West, and as well we had my Uncle Bert and his family in the Northwest Territories. Here, in one place, they could be kept up to date with how things were progressing. The outpouring of support through the words and letters we received from family and friends, and people from across Canada and the world, made us realize that we weren't really alone in this journey after all.

After the article in the Toronto Sun, a lot of people contacted me wanting to help. Old family friends, co-workers of my Dad's from years before, and complete strangers would go on to send in letters of protest for the Offender's file in Kingston. Everyone, whether they knew our family or not, agreed that the Parole Board of Canada was too lenient, and that some people just did not deserve to be out in society, that they forfeited that right upon the commission of their crimes. Words cannot adequately express how much this meant to my family and me. I had letters from people telling me about loved ones they lost through murder years before, and letters from others telling me that after the sudden loss of a loved one that their journey was just beginning. I would find out some things that were disturbing, though. I had emails from people who worked in Kingston and the surrounding area. There were a few telling me that they worked in the restaurant business, and offenders would be dropped off and not picked up again until the end of their community service workday. They were not, however, in sight and sound of Corrections as they were supposed to be. One woman would go on to tell me that Offenders would even get a cut of the tips. She said that she had no training of how to deal or how to interact with offenders; she just wanted to make a living. I also received an email from someone who said she knew that, as part of their community service, some offenders would be assigned to clean up cemeteries. As they would know where they would be at a certain time period, offenders would contact their friends or families and then pick up drugs and cash that were hidden in prearranged sites at the cemetery. I called Correctional Services Canada and passed on all the information I was receiving. Let them deal with those offenders, I thought, there was only one whom I had time for.

Every time I had a new idea, anytime before I would speak to a reporter or do any other media, there were two people whom I would run things past. I had to make sure that my Mum and my sister Caroline were all right with me being so public about things: this was not just my story but theirs as well. Caroline has always struggled with our Dad's murder, and to this day she still does. I just wanted to make sure she and her family were okay with the publicity that this story was generating. If, I told her, at any point she wanted me to stop, she was to let me know. And I would stop, for her I would. But she didn't -- she wanted me to carry on, saying that it would probably destroy me to just sit back and not do anything. Although I was the public face of this, I had the support of my family, and that was always very important to me. My mother was immensely proud of the work I was doing, and her sister, my Aunt Margy and her husband were behind me as well. I would often speak to my Aunt Jean in Charlottetown, and she would assure me that I was doing the right thing and encourage me to take the story as far as I could. My

Uncle Bert and my cousins in the Northwest Territories gave me unwavering support. And it was from these people, these family members who had known my Dad so very well, that I would draw my strength from.

That summer I would start to do something that would become a restorative habit for me. As soon as school broke up, I would pack up everything to do with the Parole Board and put it out of sight. I would shut it all away on the bottom shelves of a huge wall cabinet that was in the room where my desk was set up and where I did all my Parole Board work from. Every letter, every note I made to myself, everything that had to do with the Parole Board and Correctional Services was jammed away in that wall cabinet for the duration of the ten-week school break. And there it would stay until school resumed in September, and then I would bring it all out, sort through it, and start again where I had left off. I knew that Terry Porter and the Parole Board could not be the sole focus of my existence, and it was important that they didn't become that. I was very passionate about what I was doing, very determined and focused, but at the same time, I couldn't be obsessive about it. That, I reasoned, would be giving Terry Porter too much power. The trick, as with everything in life, was to find the right balance.

And for the first time in many years, I would travel again on my own. I needed to be in a place where I always felt happiness, where all my memories were good ones. There was only one place that I would go, and that would be to England. Back to the place I fell in love with all those years before, where I could meander along the coastline and watch the water shimmer in the morning sun and hear the laughter lapping in its waves. Where the rolling green swells of the South Downs that entranced me all those years before would charm me all over again. The unending swatches of green threaded through the fabric of the land that I love are steadfast, unchanging. The rise and fall of the downs enrapture me, and I hold them close in my mind when I am not near. Their depths mirror my own and they draw me close and embrace me; burnished brown grasslands alternating with dancing green fields that reflect the eyes that gaze upon them. Gently, the caress of the wind blows across their peaks and valleys to touch me, whispering so quietly that only I hear them say, no matter how far I go, they will wait patiently for my return.

I look in the distance toward the chalky white cliffs that stand high above the shore, their uneven heads rising majestically above the water. We are still standing, they tell me, we are still here. We may crumble and be less of ourselves as time passes, but we still stand. I journey back to England to spend time with the people who know me so well, who have been part of my life since that long ago summer when I first arrived upon her shores. Freda, Paul, Alan and I seamlessly drop back into each other's lives and effortlessly pick up where we left off as only good friends are able to do. We spend our time together laughing and reminiscing, looking back at moments we've shared and creating new ones. I spend a lot of time with these wonderful friends of mine, but I also return to England so I can be on my own, to explore my thoughts, to turn things over in my mind. Sussex is a place I can go to ponder, to think, with no distractions greater than the rise and fall of the tide and the ever-present backdrop cry of the gulls. I lost my heart to England years before, and I willingly surrender it every time I return.

England is a balm to me.

Chapter 16 ~ Dead Reckoning

By now, I was getting regular updates from the Parole Board and Correctional Services about Terry Porter. I would be told of his every transfer for medical reasons and each time he was relocated to another facility or treatment centre. I knew already about the escorted absences to Hope House in Ottawa that were granted to him at the panel hearing the year before. So I was quite surprised to receive a letter from Correctional Services regarding more escorted temporary absences for Terry Porter. Where does he want to go to now, I thought?

The letter notified me that the Warden at the offender's institution had authorized an Escorted Temporary Absence (ETA) program for the purposes of Personal Development. A Correctional Service of Canada staff member or a trained non-security escort would escort Terry Porter. He would be allowed to be absent from the institution on more than one occasion for a maximum of four hours a week in Kingston and surrounding area. And there was no end date to the ETA program.

I felt sick. Here we go again.

Terry Porter, the letter read, was granted 40 hours a month to do community service work in the Kingston and Gananoque area. And how, I asked, was this decision reached? The warden at the prison authorized it. I didn't understand; a year ago there was a panel hearing to determine if he could go out for, when compared to this, just a few hours. Now, and without the benefit of a panel hearing, he was permitted to be out in the community but on a greater scale.

If the letter from them angered me, the phone call I would make to them to clarify things incensed me. These absences, I was told, are to allow offenders to "avail themselves of rehabilitative, employment, personal and cultural activities with the goal of re-integrating them into the community and enhancing public safety." And what made it more infuriating is that I wasn't allowed to know anything else. Correctional Services wouldn't tell me what kind of community service he was performing, or what kind of setting he would be doing it in. That, they told me, would be violating his privacy. Violating HIS privacy? After what the Parole Board did to me that day the year before at the Panel Hearing? There was zero concern for my privacy then, but the convicted murderer has his privacy protected. What on earth was wrong with these people?

The conversation continued, and I asked if the people who were working alongside of him would know his past, that the offender standing beside them had axed a man to death two decades earlier? No, came the answer. Never mind me, I told them, but why was this information being withheld from the working public and the Canadian public as a whole? "What do you want us to do," they asked me, "take an ad out in the local newspaper?"

Well, yes, actually I do, I told them, but I know you won't. And, while you're at it, here's a few other ideas I have that would make your system fairer. I think there should be a current picture of Terry Porter posted somewhere. Ideally a webpage set up saying who he is, what he was convicted of and in what sector of the community he would be doing his community service in. That would be fair, as it would shift the rights of the offender back to where they belonged, to the rights of victims and the general public. Wishful thinking on my part because there would be way too many privacy breaches in regards to his rights. So, I thought, Parole Board and Corrections, while you are busy protecting Terry Porter's rights, I am going to get busy too. I spoke to Jeff Mitchell again, and Michele Mandel. The local newspaper had me on their front page, and on Monday, October 28th, 2013, the Toronto Sun surprised me by putting my picture on the front page of their paper too. In it, I'm pictured standing on the sidewalk in front of the house my dad was killed in, and I was holding the certificate of conviction from all those years before. 'LIFE' A JOKE, the headlined screamed. They even put the old mug shot of Terry Porter on the corner of the front page with the word 'killer' under it. This suited me perfectly fine as I've always felt I needed to find my way to the tallest building around here, get to the top of it and tell my story. Well, on that day and by putting me on the front page of their paper, the Toronto Sun became the tallest building for me, my CN tower. And I couldn't have done it any better even if I had climbed all of its 1,776 steps and shouted out my story from the very top of Toronto's iconic landmark.

So my story told of how, somewhere along the line, the rights of offenders have superseded the rights of victims. Not only the rights of victims, though, they have also surpassed the rights of the general public. Here I was, a hard-working, tax-paying citizen with no criminal record, and the Parole Board violated my privacy rights by telling my father's murderer my name. Yet at the same time, they were protecting Terry Porter's rights. The sheer wrongness of the whole situation infuriated me – they were protecting the wrong person.

I was incensed and I was adamant: the public should have the right to know whom the Parole Board was placing in the community. No offender is going to point that out, so it should be the Parole Board's responsibility to inform the public what is happening where they live. And look at the other side of this, think about all the high school students who need to have a certain number of community services hours completed by graduation time. There's no way I would want my children working beside someone who, unbeknownst to them, was convicted of a serious offense.

Thanks to the Internet, this story picked up

speed, and it was featured in a lot of big cities throughout Ontario. I did radio, television and more print media interviews. I was exhausted, but I still kept going because this was no longer just about me, it was about every single one of us. But, as I put it to Michele Mandel of the Sun, was it just me? I often wondered, if I was so affected by this, did it prevent me from seeing what everyone else may have been seeing? Was I too close to see things properly? Or had times changed so much in the intervening years from when my Dad was murdered, that people felt more relaxed about things, and did I fail to change along with everyone else? Was it only me who found the actions of the Parole Board and Corrections ludicrous?

No, she assured me, it wasn't just me. And judging by the correspondence I received that day and the ensuing weeks and months, she was right. The volume of support I received after my story hit the front page of the Toronto Sun was phenomenal, and I am ever grateful. To know that I was not alone in all of this made me even more determined to continue.

Well done, my son, well done.

No matter how many letters I would write, no matter how many phone calls I would make, to me it would seem that the Parole Board of Canada was answerable to no-one. They certainly weren't answerable to me, and definitely not to the Canadian public. There must be someone else I could contact, something else I could do. So I called Jade at Durham Region Victim Services to run things past her and see what she could suggest.

It was she who put me in contact with the Federal Office of Victims of Crime. The contact name I had was a woman named Julie, and she would come to be someone that I always enjoyed speaking to. I would have a ton of questions and she would answer all of them for me. I was curious, though, how a Government office like hers would be critical of another government branch -- namely the Parole Board. She assured me that they were completely independent of each other. I told her of the issues I was having with the Parole Board and what had happened in the past in regards to being named in front of my Dad's murderer. Despite the letter of regret that I received from them, I felt nothing had really changed. I gave Julie all the details I had, and she promised to look into it.

Good. Because, I found out at the beginning of this journey, it was when I stopped moving, when I stopped trying to make a difference, that was when I would feel the full weight of it all. I knew that I was never going to change the world, so I thought, how about I try to change the bit around me? Maybe I could make an easier path for others who have to go down the same road, spare them some of what I had been through.

So all the familiar feelings of stress, anger and everything else I had dealt with were coming back. I was now waking up through the night in agony: I had gone back to scrunching my shoulders up to my ears again. It got so bad that each night when I lay down in bed, I had to pull my knees to my chest and wrap my arms around my legs and sleep like that. As uncomfortable as it was, it at least kept my shoulders down. Things were starting to get on top of me again, and I didn't need anything else to deal with. Yes, I still had bad dreams, and I would often wake up in the night frozen with fear thinking that Terry Porter was out there, somewhere. I needed an outlet for my anger; somewhere I could go and try to channel things. And I found it, in the most unlikely of places that I ever thought I would find myself: a gym.

Me, in a gym? It just didn't seem possible! Gym? Wasn't the correct spelling Jim? And wasn't that the nickname of someone named James? And when I was sweating it out in one of the classes and the instructor said to do a plank, I thought Plank? Planking? Wasn't that what my husband bought at Home Depot when he fixed the deck? Up until that point in my life, I thought planking were pieces of wood. You get the picture, even to my own mind, me being anywhere near a gym seemed remote.

By going to the gym, not only did I meet a lot of fantastic people, it became part of my ritual. Most mornings I would find myself making my way there and I loved it. I loved the fast pace of the spin classes, and I took part in as many classes as I could. I did some of my best thinking on the treadmill, with my headphones on, walking many miles to nowhere. But inside I was headed somewhere because it wasn't the physical changes that I felt the most, it was the mental changes. I found something that I never really expected: Control. I might not be able to control the Parole Board or Correctional Services, but I could control something, and that was my state of mind. I may not be able to control the bad dreams and nightmares I was having, but here I could build up resilience and the mental resolve to bounce back from them quickly.

But when I would think through everything and the process with the Parole Board and Corrections, one of the very things that frightened me the most was the loss of myself. I had been through a trauma when I was younger and then, over the years, I healed somewhat and put myself back together again as best as I possibly could and got on with life. When the trauma was re-opened two decades later during the panel hearing and the weeks preceding it, it was like someone was putting a finger on the most sensitive part of a wound and re-awakened everything that caused it in the first place. And that, I worried, would jeopardize my self, my being.

So by taking control as best I could, by finding a positive outlet for my stress, and by letting good people in who were willing to help me, I was protecting myself. And in my mind, I broke it down and I would remind myself of 'self'-- the Self-Empowerment-of-Lisa-Freeman, the word self spelled out with my initials. That acronym would do a lot for the state of my mind. No matter if I didn't see immediate results from going to the gym in a physical way, I was still getting something just as important. I was building a mental resolve, not just in regards to facing the Parole Board, but for facing life in general. I may have been broken, my spirit sapped, but I would build myself up again, and the preservation of myself through this journey was paramount. So there I would be almost every day, lost amongst the muscle-sculpted bodies, dedicated fitness gurus and everyday people who were just looking to get into better shape. I would plug in my headphones and turn on the television that was part of the elliptical machine or treadmill that I happened to be on, and put on Just for Laughs Gags. This Canadian hidden-camera reality show would entertain me while I burned away my stress, laughing myself stupid over the hilarious gags, but at the same time trying to keep my concentration on whatever piece of exercise machine I happened to be on. The last thing I needed was to draw attention to myself by laughing so much that I got my feet tangled up in the machine or, God forbid, fall off of it and make a spectacle of myself.

Seriously, though, it was as if a force out there knew that I put things away for the summer and then pulled them back out to work on once September arrived. It was about midway through the month when I received a call from the Regional Victims Services Manager from Correctional Services Canada. I was informed that Correctional

226

Services were watching my Justice for Dad page, and they did not like some of the content that I had shared on there. Apparently, they didn't like it that I had informed people through my page and the media of the comings and goings of Terry Porter. I knew straight away what they were referring to, all the attention in regards to the community service work. As well, they did not like that I put on my page that he was taken involuntarily to a psych facility, only to be released into minimum security a week later.

It all comes down to confidentiality rights, again. His versus the public's and mine. Corrections then explained to me that they were concerned that I was jeopardizing the security of the facility, correctional security staff and the security of Terry Porter himself. I counted to ten. Then I told them that nowhere on their correspondence to me, and I had a lot of it, was there anything stating that I wasn't allowed to share this information. As well, I told them, it was their responsibility to maintain the security of the facility and their staff. And as for Terry Porter, I am sure that if they were to return him to his prison cell, he would be nice and secure there. Terry Porter, I said, had his rights, and I was exercising the freedom of mine. At the same time as I was fighting Terry Porter's rights and his privacy, I knew, however, that Correctional Services had a point. I worked in a data protected environment, and I know all about respecting people's confidentiality. The difference here, though, is that with anything in regards to Terry Porter, or any other offender in the system, I had a mental block. My mind would not let me get past it, it would not give him any leeway, and I was okay with that. It was just the way my mind worked, it was a default setting in my mind, and I was fine with not adjusting it. I was not willing to give one bit in regards to the man who killed my father, not an inch. As well, when it came to protected data, mine should have been protected just as much as his, if not more. After all, I wasn't the axe-swinging murderer -- he was. When you commit a crime like murder, the most capital of crimes, you should expect to forfeit a lot, not just your freedom. This didn't seem to be the case here. And it riled me. The next letter I received from Corrections was just a routine transfer that Terry Porter was making. First thing I noticed across the top of the page was a brand new confidentiality banner, stating that the contents of the letter were not to be shared. It went on to say, amongst other things, that the information contained in the letter should not be made available to the public by any means, including posting it online. I called them to clarify something. Was I the only person who was receiving letters with this banner? No, I was told, it was now standard on all communication letters.

Just checking, Corrections, just checking.

So over the next while, I would do many things in pursuit of making people aware of my Dad and my story and the challenges I was coming up against with the Parole Board. I was invited to speak in front of the criminology and victimology classes from the University Institute of Ontario. (UOIT) My first thought was, no, I can't do it, I'm not a public speaker, and I couldn't see it happening. Then there was a little voice inside my head that was prompting me, yeah, you know what? Maybe you can do it. And from there I was, yes, I will do it. I called up Professor Hannah Scott and made an appointment to meet up with her to go over things. Not only did I find my voice in regards to the Parole Board, I was applying it to other areas in my life. So as I made my way to the front of what was the old Regent Theatre from my childhood, I cleared my throat and started to speak. Was I nervous? You bet, but I had my friends Tammy and Kris in the theatre that evening for a bit of support. Actually, I had them there for a lot of support and just in case I keeled over from nervousness and stage fright, so they could come collect me off the stage and take me home.

But once I got started talking, the nervousness disappeared. After all, this was my story, I knew it inside out and I hardly needed notes. I had written down a few, though, with dates and a timeline, just to keep things straight. The most important thing I had was a note that I wrote to myself and clipped to the top of the page so I could see it when I glanced down: Act as if what you do makes a difference. It does. Because, I told these students, you never know what will happen, what change your actions might bring. I had no expectation of getting any response from the Parole Board when I started writing letters to them. For me, I just felt better by putting my feelings into words and then putting them in an envelope and sending them somewhere. It was a release: by posting my letter in a mailbox, some of the hurt and anger I was feeling went along with it. And when I received replies, I went from strength to strength: Action evokes change, I told these students, and if you believe in what you are doing, you can influence people and bring forward positive change that can benefit many others. I told the students what I kept reminding myself when I thought that things were too overwhelming: that I may not be able to change the world, but I could do the best I could to change my part of it.

The students had a lot of questions and I answered them as best as I could. Did I believe in the death penalty? No, I replied, but at times that opinion changed, depending on my mood, but for now I would be satisfied if Terry Porter spent his life behind bars. Do I think that prisoners could be rehabilitated? Some, I said, but I could only speak about the one offender I knew about. And with his past history of faked compliance and a very violent past, I didn't think he could be. Did I see in the future that I would be able to take part in a restorative justice program with this offender? I had zero interest in participating in any restorative justice program with this offender, my mind would not even entertain the thought. It was time to wrap up, but I had one more thing to say to the students. I told them that if they left the building tonight and by tomorrow they couldn't remember my name, or remember anything that I had said that evening, I was okay with that. But I asked them to remember what I was going to say next, as it was the most important information from my talk this evening. I said to just think about this: Have you ever wondered what a murder victim would say if their voices weren't silenced forever?

For the very least, the very least, they would demand that their voices are heard louder than their killer's.

A week before Christmas of 2012 and about an hour before I was due to go in for my shift at work, I received a phone call from Julie at the Ombudsman's office. It had taken time, she told me, but the National Parole Board, based on my complaint to their office, had to change its policy about what information is shared with offenders about victims of crime. The Parole Board had to make changes to their website, Victims Statement Checklists and any other means of communications that victims would have access to.

I put my head down on my desk and cried. Finally, finally, change had come. Never again would anyone ever stand at a Panel Hearing and be introduced to an Offender as I had been. The Do and Do Not list in regards to making a Victim Impact Statement would be amended. It would take time, though, and the Parole Board had a year to implement the changes, and that was fine by me. The Parole Board of Canada was righting a wrong, and by doing so, many victims of crime would be affected. All I wanted from the beginning was an acknowledgment that they were wrong in naming me in front of my father's killer, and to have them change their policies and procedures so it would not happen again to anyone else.

As time moved on, there was a steady flow of letters that would trickle in from either the Parole Board or Corrections, just to inform me of routine things. I would read them, call if I had any questions, but mostly they would just be clipped together and filed away in my desk. It was now the fall of 2014; my bags were packed and I was getting ready for my yearly solo sojourn back to England. Nick brought the mail in and there was a letter from the Parole Board. I opened it to read that Terry Porter was applying for unescorted temporary absences from the prison. I guess this was the 'baby steps' that the Parole Board kept telling me about. First he had the escorted passes, and now he wanted to be granted passes away from the prison to do, well, whatever, but he wouldn't have an escort, and I wasn't too clear on what his plans were. I was also informed that I could come to the prison in Kingston to do another Victim Impact Statement if I chose to. Oh, yes, I would choose to, I told myself. I already had one statement in the file from the previous panel hearing, but you could update one and re-submit it. Right now, though, I was going away, back to reconnect with my Sussex friends who, after so many years of friendship, were like family. I would try my best to put it to the back of my mind; it was hard to, though. Just get on with your time away, enjoy yourself, everyone told me. Right, I would, and it could all be dealt with in two weeks time when I was back in the country.

However, there was no need. When I returned, there was another letter from the Parole Board. Terry Porter, they had informed me, had withdrawn his right to unescorted temporary absences from the prison. It was his right to cancel any hearing at any time. I wondered where this was leading, what Terry Porter was up to.

Before I really had time to let that letter sink in, I received yet more correspondence from the Parole Board. It confirmed that the Offender had exercised his right to withdraw the unescorted absences; therefore, there was no need for the panel hearing that was scheduled for January 2015. Instead, however, he was to have a Full Parole review instead. And that was scheduled for January 2016.

I was not happy. Surely, I asked, he can't leap frog past things, and he can't go from escorted temporary absences to community service and then to a Full Parole review? Yes, he could, I was informed. What about the 'baby steps?' Certainly, being out in the community without an escort was a huge step, and seemingly, was that not something he was obligated to fulfill? Wouldn't it make more sense to do that before a Full Parole Review, which was a colossal step? My head was hurting and the familiar feeling of dread was soon replaced with anger and disbelief.

Because, I was wondering, just who does the Parole Board of Canada keep in prison if they are letting the axe murderers out?

So when it was time to put the yearly memoriam in the local newspaper, and just as before I wanted to honour my Dad's memory but at the same time inform the public about the policies of the Parole Board, I had to think what I could do that was different. I had to think of other ways of reaching people. I often wondered what those little computer squares were on everything that I saw. I had seen them everywhere, from the side of a medium cup container at McDonald's to the packaging of everyday household items. My husband told me that they were called QR codes and that you just scanned them with your phone and it would automatically take you to the company's link. Hmm, I wondered, did our resident teenager Kayla know how to do things like this? Maybe she could help me set one up, I thought. Nick surprised me by saying not only did he know how to do it but that he even had the QR reader app on his phone. So we got busy. I drafted an open letter to the Parole Board, telling them that I would take whatever avenue I could to tell people of the re-victimization of people through their policies and behaviours. Nick did whatever else was needed to get my letter into one of those little magic boxes. We made a mock-up of the memoriam, complete with a QR code, and sent it to the same paper that published the last memorial I put in. And it looked brilliant. I honoured my Dad by putting a list of the ships he sailed on in his Navy days and at the same time got my message across about the unfairness of the Parole Board and Corrections. I had quite a bit of reaction from the public and, again, more letters would go into Terry Porter's Offender file. Equally important was that the public was being told the extent that the Parole Board was able to divulge personal information of the very people they should be protecting. This was so very important to me because it seemed no one knew about what powers offenders had, or what powers the Parole Board gave them.

AN OPEN LETTER TO THE PAROLE BOARD OF CANADA AND CORRECTIONAL SERVICES CANADA

"I question why your organizations go to such lengths to protect Offenders' privacy. During a Panel Hearing in 2012, my full name was used twice in front of my Dad's killer. I cannot even begin to express what this did to me. I made several complaints up the chain of command, only to be told amongst other things, "that the Offender has the right to know who is complaining about him."
I am asking for reasonable change to a

system that seemingly puts the Offender's rights before the rights of people who have been victimized by their crimes. It is my understanding, that based on my complaint, the Parole Board of Canada is updating their fact sheets to reflect how a person's name can be used. I applaud this change for the sole reason that no one else will be caught unaware as I was. However, this small step is not enough.

I am asking the Government of Canada to change their archaic policies and procedures framework and guidelines. The outdated practice of using the Victim's name but removing their locator details doesn't reflect the changes in technology whereby a person's address and personal information are easily accessible to anyone. Your changes ARE NOT ENOUGH because Offenders SHOULD NOT be entitled to something as precious as a Victim's identity.

I will continue to take every avenue I can to tell the public that, through my experiences, how unfairly your system operates. How, with the assistance of the Parole Board of Canada and Correctional Services Canada, Victims of Crime are victimized not only by the Offender but by your organizations as well. PRIVACY RIGHTS SHOULD NOT BE JUST A 'RIGHT' FOR THE OFFENDER, BUT FOR EVERYONE."

*****

As I put these letters and my thoughts about the Parole Board and Correctional Services Canada on my Justice for Dad page I often wondered about those government branches that were watching my site. I know there were a lot of people in the media who had the link to it, and because of the complaint I had earlier about posting confidential information, I knew these government bodies were watching my page. Instead of going on a rant about them, I instead welcomed them to my page and thanked them for their interest in it. I had my tongue firmly planted in my cheek when I typed that I hoped that they were learning something by watching it and reading what I was posting. And, if they were open to suggestions, please by all means, contact me.

Coincidentally, I had heard about Prime Minister Stephen Harper's Life Means Life bill not long after. This bill would see people who were convicted of first degree murder actually serve a life sentence. The bill would target those convicted of murders that involve kidnapping, sexual assault, terrorism, or the killing of police officers and correctional officers. As well, it would remove the possibility of parole for the most brutal of murderers. I thought about the Certificate of Conviction that was handed to me almost two-and-a-half decades before. That was a federal document, sentencing a man to Life Imprisonment with no parole eligibility for twenty-five years. What, I wondered, was the difference between now and then? Except that the document I had held no worth.

That wasn't right. When we told our daughters about the Full Parole review that would be coming up in 2016, my youngest girl, who was now 9, said, "I thought he was supposed to be in jail for life?" I said well, that's what the piece of paper says, but that's not what is happening. She said, "Well, that's like they are lying."

Out of the mouth of babes.

The Conservative Government and their proposed Life Means Life bill was in the news a lot. And over and over again, I read news stories of how offenders are currently sentenced to life with no parole eligibility for 25 years. Wrong, wrong, wrong, I would think, parole starts way before that. I wasn't far wrong in saying that it was a common misconception by most people that the parole process doesn't start till the twenty-five-year mark of a sentence. So it was continuously misreported everywhere I looked and on every newscast that I happened to be watching. So I thought I should try to correct a few people beginning with a reporter from Canada's biggest national newspaper, the Globe and Mail. I pointed out that his paper was misguiding the public, and he heard me out and agreed to meet with me, and for a few hours I shared my story with him. The Canadian Broadcasting Corporation (CBC) continued to rile me, and I left a message on a toll-free number line telling them that they were wrong and they really shouldn't be aiding the Parole Board by reporting misinformation.

That was a Friday, and by Monday I had completely forgotten about it. It just felt better to say something; even if no one was going to pay any attention, I felt better by correcting a few people. So when the producer of Matt Galloway's Radio Talk Show CBC Morning called, I told her she didn't really have to speak to me. I had my rant on her answering machine and I felt better for it. She asked me some questions, I told her about some of the things that I had been through, and she asked if I could come into Toronto to be a guest on the morning show. And so I did, catching the early morning GO train into Toronto on a dark and chilly spring morning. As I waited for my turn to go on air, I was nervous but determined. Matt asked me to tell him and his listeners a bit of my Dad's story and what prompted me to call the CBC a few days before. So I gently corrected the CBC on air about the misinformation given by most media when stating that a life sentence in Canada means no parole for 25 years, and that they would do a greater service to people and families like mine if the facts were accurately reported. He agreed and then asked me what I thought about the hot topic of the proposed bill in regards to keeping the most dangerous of criminals away from the public. I was in full support of it, of course, but I also challenged Prime Minister Stephen Harper to put his money where his mouth is in regards to this new bill. By having Life mean Life for new offenders who were sentenced to Life Imprisonment, to make our country safer for Canadians, he should take it further. Make the new legislation retroactive; put a clause in for those brutal murderers currently incarcerated in prison. Have Life mean Life for them as well. If you want a safer Canada, Mr. Harper, keep dangerous prisoners that are already incarcerated behind bars right where they are.

I also wrote letters to the Prime Minister, Justice Minister Peter MacKay and Minister of Public Safety Steven Blaney asking why a murderer convicted of first degree murder now should be treated any differently from the man who murdered my father all those years ago. Certainly, I said, there should be some consistency through the years and with such a serious matter. If life is going to mean life now, why not honour the federal certificate of conviction from years before that clearly states a sentence of life? Each person I wrote to handed it off to the other – the Prime Minister's Office to Justice MacKay, and Justice MacKay to Steven Blaney. I am still waiting to hear a reply from Mr. Blaney. I note that it was only through the intervention of my local Member of Parliament, Colin Carrie, that I received any replies to my first letters at all. I condensed my meeting with Colin into a letter and sent it to him querying why I hadn't received any replies from those I sent letters to. He then forwarded to the different ministers on my behalf and only then did I receive replies.

By going on Matt Galloway's radio show that morning, did anything I say or propose make a difference? Did it change anything in the way the CBC reported parole eligibility? I don't know, but if I can be on Toronto's number one morning radio show and tell the general public about the misconception of no parole until the twenty-five-year mark, then I was more than happy to do so.

There were so many things that the Parole Board told me that I would still not agree with, and one of those things was that panel hearings were not about the victims but rather about the offenders and their progress in regards to rehabilitation. I still say that there must be some room made for the victim and the acts committed by the offender. By just looking at the man and the time spent in prison since committing the crime, I argued that they were only looking at the surface of the person. To see their greater depth, just as when looking at an iceberg, you must look beneath the surface to see what lies under there, to see what is lurking. So how do you measure the depth of someone? You look at the whole picture. And in this case, I think that graphic details and images of the crime should be revisited at panel hearings. Everyone has heard the saying that a picture speaks a thousand words, but the Parole Board was very clear, there were to be no graphic images sent in. Not that I had any from the crime scene, of course, just the one of my Dad in the morgue that is forever etched in my mind. It's locked away, but my mind works like a filing cabinet. I can just open a drawer, pull out the file, and it will be there, just as clear and detailed as it was the first time I saw it. I could stand up at a panel hearing and describe for everyone what I had seen, and I had done so, but that was never going to be enough. What else could I do, I thought, what else could I get in that file to have people, these panelists, see the true depth of Terry Porter and his violent nature? And then it came to me -- the coroner's report. I wondered how long the Coroner's Office kept their records? This crime happened almost 25 years ago, what were the chances?

As it turned out, the chances were very good. I spoke to someone at the Coroner's Office in Toronto, and they gave me a name and number for the East Division. I called them and explained who I was and what I was interested in. And much to my shock, they told me they kept the records for fifty years. Fifty years! Could I get a copy after all this time? Yes, I could, and it arrived a few weeks later. My thinking was that if I could get a copy of the coroner's report, I could try to get it submitted into Terry Porter's file. Even though it wasn't pictures, the coroner's words would have some impact and would tell the brutality of the crime and the rage behind my father's wounds. Best of all, it wouldn't be just my words in that file describing the attack on my father, the coroner's words would be there too.

The thick envelope arrived from the coroner's office on my birthday. I set it aside and enjoyed my special day. But the very next day I opened up the envelope and sat down and braced myself to read back to almost twenty-four years before to see what the Coroner saw and reported with his words.

There was never any doubt about the brutality of the attack on my father by Terry Porter. I had seen my Dad's body at the morgue and I had seen the crime scene when my sister and I tried to clean it up a few days after the murder. So a lot of what I read in the report from the Coroner I knew already. However, what I gained from the detailed report was insight to the absolute savagery of Terry Porter's attack.

I read the detailed forensics report outlining where they matched Terry Porter's hair to the ones found at the crime scene. They collected and listed the items that Terry Porter was wearing the evening he killed my father -- tan boots, black jacket, blue jeans and a blue sweatshirt. When the hairs and contaminant fibres were removed and analyzed, they consisted of animal hairs, human body hair, and human hair. They forensically compared the fibres of the carpet in the room to the fibres that were recovered from what Terry Porter was wearing. And it all matched. It was both fascinating reading and sickening reading all at the same time.

Items reported to be from the scene were noted beside a list of hairs. Hairs by the leg of the brown chair. Hairs by the front of the Dexter hat. Hairs between the hat and the green chair, as well as hairs on the blue harbour hat. Hairs on a black vinyl case and hairs on a plant stand. What, I thought, did they have to list every hair found in the room? That would be an impossible task and one that could never be finished, as there are hairs everywhere.

In the summary and conclusion section of the report, the Coroner stated that in the items reported to be from the scene, those items consist of scalp hair clumps containing from twenty to well in excess of one hundred hairs. The hairs from these items are microscopically similar to the known sample, item B89 (SLINGERLAND). The root condition of the hairs are indicative of forceful removal from the scalp. The coroner's report spoke volumes of the brutality from that evening long ago.

This was repeated all through the report, that clumps of hair found in that room were pulled out from the scalp by force. These clumps were found everywhere in that room, on the furniture, on clothing, on a plant stand. The words were repeated and often underlined. Pulled out by force. The image in my mind and the terror my father must have felt when he was beaten by Terry Porter was hard to shake. Terry Porter was an animal, I have always known that, and what I saw in the morgue that long ago night wasn't done by a human but by an out-of-control beast. And reading the coroner's report from almost twenty-five years before confirmed it. It wasn't pleasant reading, but I reminded myself that Terry Porter couldn't hurt my Dad anymore, and he hadn't hurt him for a long time. And I had built my mind up and my mental resolve so much that, I hoped, he couldn't hurt me anymore either.

Knowing as I did from the first Panel Hearing in January of 2012, anything that is in the Offender's file has to be read, by law, by the panelists for the hearing and by the offender himself. I wanted the Parole Board and Terry Porter to know that I was doing everything possible to keep him in prison. And if I could keep him in prison even one hour more than he thought he would be, then I would be successful in my mission.

So I made copies of the letters I wrote to the Prime Minister and the other ministers and their replies and sent them to the Parole Board to be included in Terry Porter's file. To my surprise, they accepted them without objection, without a fight.

I made a copy of the Coroner's report and submitted it to the Parole Board for inclusion in Terry Porter's file. I am pleased to say that the report was again accepted without objection and placed into the file and will be read by the panelists prior to the panel hearing for Full Parole Review in January 2016. And just in case Terry Porter forgot how brutal his extended attack was, by law, he has to read it as well. You can fool some people, Terry Porter, but you cannot fool me -- I saw what you did to my father. These panelists and the people who support you now in your life have no idea of the monster you really are. I will do whatever I can, whatever I need to do to give them a clearer picture of you, an accurate measure of the man you are. And I'll make sure my father's voice, in whatever way I can, will be heard just as loud as yours.

I received a huge white envelope from Julie at the Federal Ombudsman's office. In it was a letter stating that my complaint to their office was used as a case example in their annual report for the year of 2013-14. This annual report was recently tabled in Parliament, and she included a copy of it for me to keep. I felt something stir inside of me, something that I let myself feel for just a short time: pride.

Is this over? No, and it never will be. In murdering my father, Terry Porter handed me and my family a cruel life sentence from which we will never be paroled. If we have to carry out a life sentence, why shouldn't Terry Porter? By his actions all those years ago, we were plunged unasked into a nightmare. And, as the years have passed, the damage he has done has inflicted every subsequent generation as well, creating a domino effect of fear and grief. When I think about his full parole bid and the enormity of it, I get worried. And scared. Throughout my life, any problems and obstacles that have come my way, I've always tried to put them into context. Instead of looking at the whole picture, or the whole problem, I would try to break them down into manageable, copeable pieces. But the prospect of Terry Porter getting full parole is something that I cannot break down. It is just too big. The release date that had always just been numbers on a piece of paper have now taken on a life of their own. He'll be able to get out, and soon. Then the enormity of it hits me: Terry Porter is entitled to full parole. And that frightens me. I don't want to be frightened, I tell myself, I want to be prepared. I need to prepare my mind now, so it has time to absorb things, to help buffer the reality of it.

In January 2016 John Terrance Porter was entitled to a Full Parole review twenty-five years into the life sentence he received for murdering my father. A few months before the end of 2015, I received a notification in the mail that he waived his right to his full review, and I can only speculate at the reasons behind this as no explanation was given. Further reading of the letter informed me that the next scheduled Full Parole review would be in December of 2020. My initial thoughts were of relief; and even though I didn't know why he waived the review, it didn't really matter -- he would have to wait at least another four years before he can proceed to another full parole review. My sense of elation was short-lived as the very next sentence told me that he has the right to apply for another full parole review at any time -- he didn't have to wait until 2020 after all.

Why, I asked the Parole Board, were they wasting my time? Why write me a letter stating the date of the next scheduled review when in reality a new date could happen at any time, and at the Offender's request? In my eyes, it should be mandatory that the man who killed my father should have to wait until the next scheduled review, or at the very least be made to wait a minimum two-year period before re-applying. After all, it was he who waived the hearing in the first place. So, instead of being able to tell my family to rest easy, that we have at least four years of peace, instead I must tell them that the Parole Board continues to be offender driven. And, because it is, we won't even know the date of a new Full Parole review until Terry Porter decides it.

One thing is certain. When it is decided, I will be ready.

We will be ready.

*****

The golden sun dips low in the evening sky, momentarily suspended on an invisible string before it sinks below the horizon; another summer evening coming to a close, another hot day beginning to cool. I close my eyes and think back along the road I've been on over the past few years and reflect upon all I've been through. The wounds of my father's murder, the ones that were never to completely heal, I thought were far enough from the surface that they would never re-open and be made to bleed again, but bleed I did. Am I a victim of Terry Porter's, have I become one? No, I tell myself -- I am not a victim.

Nor will I ever be: I am a survivor.

Well done, my son, well done.

Chapter 17 ~ Wind Travels in the Direction of the Shooting Star

Am I still that happy girl of my childhood? Yes, I am. Lessons learned early in my life have taught me that no one owns tomorrow; we can hope for it, plan for it, and at times even dread it, but no one truly owns it. John Terrance Porter may have stolen my Dad from me, but not my happy self. She is still there.

And I've found that my father and my sister haven't gone too far away after all. They are kept alive in the stories that my mother tells, and in the stories, too, from my Aunt Margy and my Aunt Jean. Their words bring them back to life again. I can feel them around me, but I can't quite reach them.

I see them all the time, too; they keep surfacing when I least expect it. I see them in the faces of my children, my sisters and my nieces. A ripple of laughter, or a passing look that will fleetingly cross their face and I see traces of long ago people there. There is a pang of sadness, of course, and a longing to have them back again in their rightly places in the world.

Our world.

And a wish that they could see who I've become and what I've become. And I wonder if I were to go a few streets over, and if I were to stand very still at the crossroads of my childhood and the present day, maybe, just maybe, if the wind is traveling in the direction of the shooting star, they'll tell me that they know.

They already know.

Epilogue

In May 2016, Lisa Freeman began a petition to the House of Commons in Ottawa, Canada, to amend certificates of conviction so they better reflect truth in sentencing.

Petition to the Government of Canada

Whereas: Certificates of Conviction are improperly worded and misleading to the general public and victims of crime;

The reality is that certain forms of parole eligibility start at the 21 year mark of a life sentence, not at the 25 year mark;

A sentence of life in prison without parole is generally understood to mean that the offender will not be eligible for any form of release for 25 years;
A proper understanding of parole eligibility should be the right of both victim(s) and offenders.

We, the undersigned, Residents of Canada, call upon the Honourable Minister of Justice and the Government of Canada to Amend the wording of Certificates of Conviction to include clarification of eligibility for all forms of parole; and mandate inclusion of an information package outlining the various forms of parole. Truth in sentencing should begin with these certificates.

The petition is open for signatures until September 27, 2016. After that date, her local Member of Parliament, Colin Carrie, will present it on her behalf to the House of Commons.

Please sign the petition at:

https://petitions.parl.gc.ca/en/Petition/Details? Petition=e-378

Thank you

A heartfelt thank you to all the good people who surround me. My family for their support, my publisher Dr. RJ Parker, and namely:

Greg O'Driscoll
Rod MacDonald
Randy Evans
Freda Moon
Paul Gower
Alan Gower
Sonia Gyrmov Bolianatz
Jean DesRoches
Bert Duford
Howard Shea
Margy and Omar Somers
Preston and Lillian Stewart
Tammy Gay
Kim Hosey
Jaqueline Martin
John and Kay O'Doherty
Donna Birkett
Hannah Scott
Monica Lancaster
David Thow
Jeff Mitchell
Chris Simmons
Janice Doore

Sheila and Gary Egmore
Philippa and David Moore
Marlene Ashard
Harold Koehler
Michele Mandel
Leigh Abbott
Jade Harper and staff of Durham Victim Services
Colin Carrie
Sean Fine
Eric Guernsey
Janice Calder
Phil Armitage
JW

And to my big sister Deb…..the best ghost writer
out there!

Thank you to my editor, proofreaders, and cover artist for your support:

~ Lisa

Aeternum Designs (book cover)

Bettye McKee (editor)

Lee Knieper Husemann

Lorrie Suzanne Phillippe

Marlene Fabregas

Darlene Horn

Ron Steed

Katherine McCarthy

Robyn MacEachern

Kathi Garcia

Linda H. Bergeron

About the Author

Lisa Freeman's passionate efforts to bring reasonable change to the Policies and Procedures of the Parole Board of Canada has inadvertently led her to be an outspoken advocate of Victim's Rights. Her story has been widely shared in newspapers across Canada and her battle with the Parole Board has led to front page coverage by the Toronto Sun. She has been a guest multiple times on CBC radio and television, as well as Newstalk Radio 1010 Toronto, and Matt Galloway's Radio One Morning show. Lisa is a regular speaker at the University of Ontario Institute of Technology (UOIT) and has spoken at various Durham Victim Services events. She remains unwavering in her stance that the rights of victims of crime should be equal to or greater than the rights of offenders.

Lisa works in the Long-Term Health Care sector and lives in the Greater Toronto Area (GTA) with her husband, two daughters, and Whiskey their German Shepherd.

Contact Lisa

http://www.authorlisafreeman.com/

shewontbesilenced@gmail.com

http://www.facebook.com/justice4dad

A portion from the proceeds of this book will be donated to Victim Services of Durham Region and St. Vincent Pallotti's Kitchen. Interested in learning more about the Halifax Explosion? Go to

www.cbc.ca/halifaxexplosion

Useful phone numbers and links

Ontario Network of Victim Service Providers
http://www.victimservicesontario.ca/

Canadian Victims Bill of Rights
http://laws-lois.justice.gc.ca/eng/acts/C-23.7/page-
1.html

Financial Assistance for Families of Homicide
Victims Program (FAFHV)
1(855) 467-4344

https://www.attorneygeneral.jus.gov.on.ca/english/o
vss/financial_assistance_for_families_of_homicide_
victims/

Office for Victims of Crime
1(877) 435-7661
www.ovc.gov.on.ca

Victim Support Line
1(888) 579-2888

Criminal Injuries Compensation Board
1(800) 372-7463
www.cicb.gov.on.ca

Legal Aid Ontario

1(800) 668-8258
www.legalaid.on.ca
Federal Parole Board
1(800) 518-8817
www.pbc.clcc.gc.ca

Ontario Review Board
1(866) 289-1667
www.orb.on.ca

Office of the Chief Coroner
1(877) 991-9959
www.ontario.ca/safety

Federal Ombudsman for Victims of Crime
1(866) 481-8429
www.victimsfirst.gc.ca

National Office for Victims
1(866) 525-0554
www.publicsafety.gc.ca

Policy Centre for Victims' Issues
www.victimsmatter.gc.ca

Made in the USA
Charleston, SC
09 December 2016